A Word A Day
Intermediate

A Word a Day provides a structured f[...] help students build vocabulary on a daily basis. Each of the 366 lessons contains the following features:

Part of Speech The part of speech is given for each word.

Contextualized Sentence Each new word is used in context, in a sentence. Each sentence is designed to provide enough context about the new word that students can easily grasp its meaning.

Definition
Each entry word is defined with a simple phrase, as in dictionaries used by intermediate students.

Critical Attributes
To help students better understand and articulate exactly what the new word means, these exercises require them to distinguish those features that are attributes of the target word from those that are not.

A Word a Day

barricade

1. verb
   to block off
2. noun
   a barrier used to block passage

The fire department had to **barricade** the streets for the parade. They parked their fire trucks across the crosswalks to make a **barricade**.

Copy and complete this Venn diagram for **barricade**:

barricade (v)   barricade (n)

When are **barricades** used to block city streets?

Synonyms and Antonyms
For some entries, familiar synonyms or antonyms are provided to further enhance comprehension.

Graphic Organizers
For some new words, students are asked to complete graphic organizers that help build a deeper understanding of word meanings.

Personal Connection
For each new word, students are asked to share an opinion, personal experience, or other comment that demonstrates their understanding of the new word. Connecting new information to previous experience facilitates learning.

Multiple-Meaning Entries
Two definitions are provided for some multiple-meaning words. Both words are used in contextualized sentences which are often related. Venn diagrams accompany many of these entries to help students focus on similarities and differences in word meanings.

How to Use

Intermediate

Scheduling

The one-a-day format is flexible enough to fit into your daily schedule in many ways. Consider any of the following:

- Introduce a new word each morning as part of your opening activities.
- Present a new word as a warm-up activity before beginning reading and language arts instruction.
- Conduct activities as a way to provide focus during transition times.
- Copy and send home to involve families in language development at home.

Presenting the Entries

To use the **Word a Day** activities in class, you may:

- Make overhead transparencies to present each of the new vocabulary words. Read aloud the word and its definition, as well as the contextualized sentence. You may continue to refer to the text on the overhead as you conduct the critical-attribute and personal-experience activities. This approach will be appreciated by all students who are visual learners.
- Read the entry for each word aloud to your class, and conduct the activities as strictly oral activities. In this case, you should write the word on the chalkboard so that students will have a visual association for it. This will allow both auditory and visual learners multiple ways in which to process the new information.
- If you wish to help strengthen students' ability to work in both auditory and visual modes, alternate your mode of presentation of the **Word a Day** entries.

Tips for Conducting the Activities

- When you conduct critical-attribute activities, be sure to call on different students to respond to the five choices in each exercise. By calling on students at random, you keep the lesson moving and the students engaged.

- Invite more than one student to respond to any of the five choices in the critical-attribute exercises, or to the personal-experience exercise. Ask the group if anybody came up with a different response, or had a different way of thinking about the exercise. Be sure students explain their answers or use logic to support their statements. When students explain their thinking, you or your students may learn that there is more than one way to look at any given exercise.

- To conduct graphic organizer activities, copy the organizer onto chart paper or the board, or use the templates on pages 187–189 to create transparencies, then work with students to complete each organizer. Encourage group participation and discussion as you work with them.

- During group discussions, remind students to be courteous listeners, giving full attention to the speaker. When unusual or minority opinions are expressed, remind students that each person is entitled to hold his or her own opinion. Encourage students to defend their opinions with logic. (This should help unusual opinions gain acceptance.)

Extending Learning

- Create "word walls" or bulletin boards on which you collect new words and organize them according to categories such as "descriptive words," "synonyms," "antonyms," and any other categories you or students identify.

- Encourage students to be on the lookout for **Word a Day** words that appear in other text that they read. You may wish to collect examples of contextualized usage, or even offer a prize for the person who finds the most **Word a Day** words in their weekly reading.

- Students who speak another language might enjoy creating dual-language dictionaries that list words in their native language that mean the same thing as the **Word a Day** entries.

A Word a Day

luminous

adjective

giving off light

The full moon was so **luminous** that Tim did not need a flashlight to see the path.

Which of these manufactured objects are **luminous**?

- a burning candle
- a fountain
- a fluorescent light
- a telephone
- a flashing camera

What are some **luminous** objects that are found in nature?

belligerent

adjective

hostile; wanting to fight

The Peace Makers at our school use conflict resolution to help stop **belligerent** behavior.

Copy and complete this word map for **belligerent**:

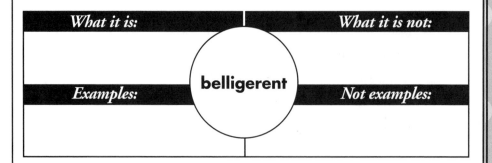

What it is:		*What it is not:*
Examples:	**belligerent**	*Not examples:*

How do you feel when someone becomes **belligerent**? What do you do? What situations make you feel **belligerent**? How do you handle those situations?

A Word a Day, Intermediate • EMC 2718 • ©2002 by Evan-Moor Corp.

elated

adjective

filled with joy

antonym: miserable

Jessica felt **elated** when she crossed the finish line first.

Which of these might you do if you felt **elated**?

- sleep
- jump
- cheer
- yawn
- smile

Tell about some events in your life that made you feel **elated**.

deceive

verb

to make someone believe something that is not true; to trick

synonym: lie

The wolf tried to **deceive** Little Red Riding Hood by dressing like her grandmother.

Which words mean about the same thing as **deceive**?

- mislead
- verify
- confirm
- falsify
- receive

Did anyone ever **deceive** you? How did it make you feel? Do you think it's ever OK to **deceive** someone else?

A Word a Day

absurd

adjective

without good sense

synonym: silly

It was **absurd** to try to eat the broth with a fork!

Which words mean about the same thing as **absurd**?

- crazy
- reasonable
- foolish
- normal
- nonsensical

What do you do that others think is **absurd**?

vanquish

verb

to defeat; overcome

synonym: conquer

Zack had to **vanquish** his fear of the dark before going camping with his friends.

Which scenarios describe somebody **vanquishing** someone or something?

- two runners cross the finish line at the same moment
- a tennis player beats her opponent
- a person with a learning disability gets all A's
- a baseball team finishes the season in last place
- a knight knocks the other rider off his horse in a jousting match

What are some fears you would like to **vanquish**? Why?

A Word a Day, Intermediate • EMC 2718 • ©2002 by Evan-Moor Corp.

A Word a Day

remedy

1. noun

   a medicine or treatment used for healing

2. verb

   to return something to its proper condition

Adam's mother gave him mint tea as a **remedy** for his upset stomach. She hoped it would **remedy** his stomachache quickly.

Copy and complete this Venn diagram for **remedy**:

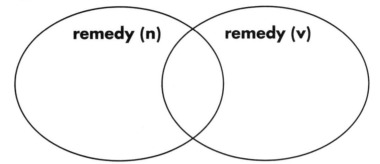

What kind of **remedies** does your family use? What conditions do you try to **remedy** with them?

bedlam

noun

a scene of noise and confusion

There was **bedlam** on the decks of the *Titanic* when the ship began to sink.

Which of these events might cause **bedlam**?

- an earthquake destroys a neighborhood
- a snake gets loose in the classroom
- a bouquet of flowers is delivered
- a fire hydrant floods a city street
- a poet reads her work at a bookstore

Imagine a scene of **bedlam**. Describe what is happening and what caused it.

A Word a Day

casual

adjective

1. happening by chance; not planned
2. informal; not fancy

When Jared's **casual** meeting with a friend led to a dinner invitation, he was glad his **casual** clothes were neat and clean.

Copy and complete this Venn diagram for **casual**:

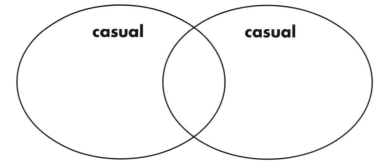

What kinds of **casual** clothes do you own? Do you like to wear them? Why or why not?

cantankerous

adjective

hard to get along with

synonym: cranky

It was hard to play with Jerry because he was so **cantankerous**.

Which words describe a person who is **cantankerous**?

- snappy
- agreeable
- crabby
- pleasant
- grouchy

What type of behavior might Jerry have displayed? How do you feel when you are around a **cantankerous** person?

A Word a Day, Intermediate • EMC 2718 • ©2002 by Evan-Moor Corp.

affluent

adjective

having a lot of money

synonym: wealthy

Marta loved to visit her **affluent** aunt because she had a swimming pool and a tennis court.

Which words mean about the same as **affluent**?

- poor
- rich
- broke
- well-off
- desperate

If you were **affluent**, what special things might you own? How might you help others if you were **affluent**?

hermit

noun

a person who lives alone in a lonely or isolated place

The **hermit** saw other people only when he hiked into town to buy groceries.

Copy and complete this concept map for **hermit**:

Examples: *Other Ways to Say It:*

hermit

Why might somebody choose to be a **hermit**? Do you think you would like to be a **hermit**? Why?

A Word a Day

dapper

adjective

attractive in dress

synonym: fashionable

James was such a **dapper** dresser that he looked like a model.

Which words describe someone who is **dapper**?

- stylish
- trendy
- drab
- sloppy
- classy

Think of famous people who are **dapper** dressers. Who would you most want to dress like?

abscond

verb

to run away secretly and hide

The bank robbers planned to **abscond** with thousands of dollars.

Copy and complete this concept map for **abscond**:

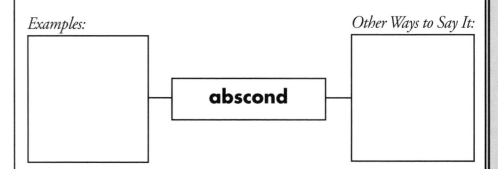

Examples:

abscond

Other Ways to Say It:

If you planned to **abscond**, where would you go?

A Word a Day, Intermediate • EMC 2718 • ©2002 by Evan-Moor Corp.

curtail

verb

to cut short; reduce

synonym: to shorten

Jeff's teacher suggested he **curtail** the time he spent playing video games if he wanted to do better on his homework.

Which activities might you **curtail** to improve your schoolwork?

- watching television at night
- paying attention in class
- staying up late on school nights
- doing homework
- reading books

List some activities you should **curtail** if you want to stay healthy.

dejected

adjective

low in spirits

synonym: discouraged

Hiroshi felt **dejected** when he didn't break the record for the long jump.

Copy and complete this concept map for **dejected**:

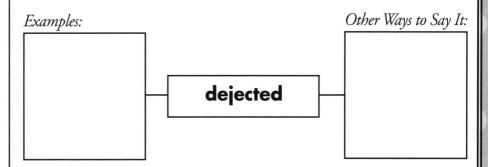

Examples: *Other Ways to Say It:*

dejected

What makes you feel **dejected**? What makes you feel better when you are feeling **dejected**?

A Word a Day

digress

verb

to get off the subject, especially when speaking or writing

The teacher took a moment to **digress** and told a funny story before getting back to the lesson.

Which of these do you do when you **digress**?

- focus
- lose track
- concentrate
- wander
- get distracted

Why might it be important not to **digress** when you are working in a group to complete an assignment? Can it ever be valuable to **digress**?

heirloom

noun

a valued article handed down from generation to generation

Alana's gold locket was a family **heirloom** that had belonged to her great-grandmother.

Copy and complete this word map for **heirloom**:

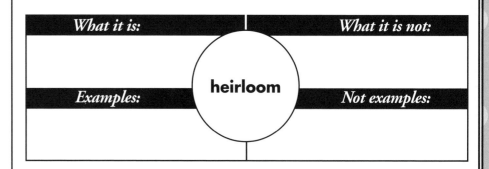

Tell about any **heirlooms** that have been passed down for generations in your family. What do you own that you might like to pass on as an **heirloom**?

A Word a Day, Intermediate • EMC 2718 • ©2002 by Evan-Moor Corp.

gregarious

adjective

happy to be with others

synonym: sociable

Because Heather was so **gregarious**, she always had friends around her.

Which of these traits would a **gregarious** person display?

- moody
- friendly
- likeable
- pleasant
- mean

Do you consider yourself to be **gregarious**? Why or why not?

docile

adjective

easy to handle or train

Anita's **docile** dog won the prize for "best-behaved pet" at the show.

Copy and complete this concept map for **docile**:

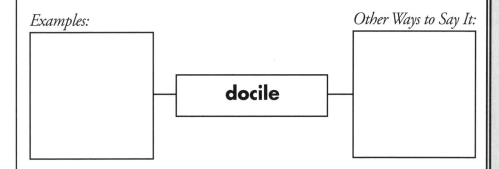

Examples: *Other Ways to Say It:*

docile

What type of behavior do you think Anita's **docile** dog exhibited to be named "best-behaved pet"? Do you prefer **docile** or lively pets?

A Word a Day

brawl

noun

a loud fight

When the pitcher accidentally hit the batter with a fastball, a **brawl** broke out between the two teams.

Which of these things might you see in a **brawl**?

- punching
- greeting
- kicking
- singing
- laughing

What are other situations in which you might see a **brawl**? What would you do if a **brawl** started near you?

germinate

verb

to begin to grow

synonym: to sprout

The spring rains helped the seeds to **germinate**.

Copy and complete this word map for **germinate**:

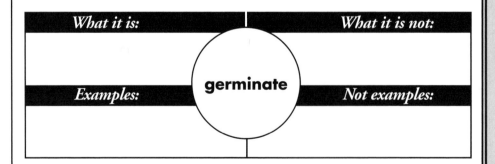

What it is:		*What it is not:*
	germinate	
Examples:		*Not examples:*

What are some of the things you can you do to help seeds **germinate**?

A Word a Day, Intermediate • EMC 2718 • ©2002 by Evan-Moor Corp.

classify

verb

to put into groups according to a system

Lilia had to **classify** the insects in her collection by color.

Copy and complete this word map for **classify**:

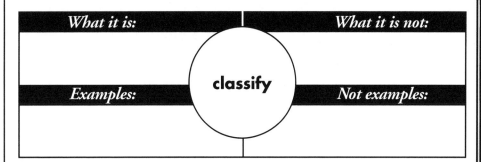

What it is:		What it is not:
	classify	
Examples:		Not examples:

Name some of your favorite foods and **classify** them into these categories: dairy products, vegetables, fruits, grains, and proteins and legumes.

tedious

adjective

boring; tiresome

Three hours of weeding a garden can be **tedious**.

How might you feel when you are doing something **tedious**?

- jolly
- tired
- excited
- weary
- energetic

What is something **tedious** that you have to do at home?

A Word a Day

admonish

verb

to give a stern warning

Mrs. Wu had to **admonish** her students about running in the hallway.

Which of these are examples of **admonishing** someone?

- A police officer stops a driver but does not write a ticket.
- A judge sentences a criminal to a year in prison.
- A mother says that next time, her child will go to the "time out" chair.
- A principal talks to students about walking their bikes at school.
- A father doesn't pay attention when his children tease each other.

Pretend that you are a parent. Your children have just come inside with mud all over their shoes. What would you say to **admonish** them?

foreign

adjective

1. from another country
2. different; not fitting in

We served lots of **foreign** foods at the international celebration. The hamburgers looked **foreign** alongside all the other exotic foods.

Copy and complete this Venn diagram for **foreign**:

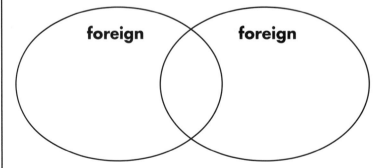

What are some of your favorite **foreign** foods?

A Word a Day, Intermediate • EMC 2718 • ©2002 by Evan-Moor Corp.

gallery

noun

a room or building where art is shown or sold

Ima was impressed by all the colorful paintings in the **gallery**.

Which of these items might you find displayed in a **gallery**?

- paintings
- envelopes
- sculptures
- photographs
- shovels

If you could see any type of exhibit in a **gallery**, what would you choose to see?

harass

verb

to bother repeatedly

synonym: to torment

My brother shoots rubber bands at me when he wants to **harass** me.

Copy and complete this word map for **harass**:

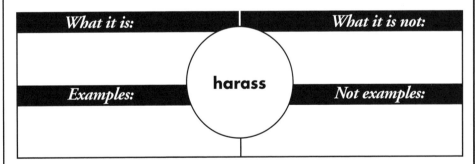

What are appropriate ways to respond to someone who is **harassing** you?

A Word a Day

indulge

verb

to give in to something for pleasure

Adrianne fought the urge to **indulge** her craving for the rich chocolate dessert.

Which of these might you feel when you **indulge** in something?

- enjoyment
- sorrow
- excitement
- fear
- pleasure

What activities do you **indulge** in for pleasure? What activities do you resist **indulging** in?

destitute

adjective

without food, shelter, or money

The fifth-graders raised money to help **destitute** people in their community.

Copy and complete this concept map for **destitute**:

Examples:

destitute

Other Ways to Say It:

What can we do to help those who are **destitute**?

A Word a Day, Intermediate • EMC 2718 • ©2002 by Evan-Moor Corp.

jumble

verb

to mix up into a confused mess

You should **jumble** the puzzle pieces before you put them away.

Which of the following describe what you do when you **jumble** something?

- put it into disorder
- organize it
- make a mess of it
- put it in its proper place
- create chaos

Tell whether you like having things in your room in a **jumble** and why.

lecture

1. noun

   a prepared talk about something

2. verb

   to scold

The park ranger gave a **lecture** about wild animals. He also had to **lecture** some campers about leaving food out for the bears.

Copy and complete this Venn diagram for **lecture**:

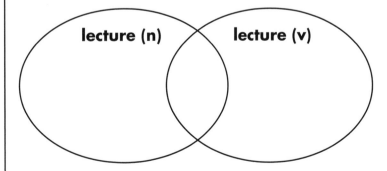

lecture (n)   lecture (v)

Tell about the subject of a **lecture** you have heard before.

A Word a Day

maneuver

verb

to move skillfully or cleverly

Mika tried to **maneuver** his bike around the cones on the obstacle course.

In which of these situations would a driver need to **maneuver** with caution?

- during a heavy rainstorm
- driving on a flat, dry road
- late at night on an empty street
- driving down an icy mountain pass
- on a city street crowded with cars, bikes, and pedestrians

Describe a situation in which you had to **maneuver** carefully.

frantic

adjective

very excited with worry or fear

Lihn was so **frantic** that she would be late, she ran all the way to school.

Copy and complete this concept map for **frantic**:

Examples: *Other Ways to Say It:*

frantic

Tell about a time when you were **frantic**. How did you feel? What did you do? Why were you **frantic**?

A Word a Day, Intermediate • EMC 2718 • ©2002 by Evan-Moor Corp.

peer

noun

a person of the same age or ability level

Even though Daisy is Roberto's **peer**, she is three inches taller than he is.

Which of these people would be your **peer**?

- your mother
- students in your class
- your grandfather
- the kids on your baseball team
- your best friend

Name three of your **peers** and three of your parents' **peers**.

stagnant

adjective

not active, changing, or developing

synonym: sluggish

The **stagnant** water in the puddle was filled with mosquito larvae.

Copy and complete this concept map for **stagnant**:

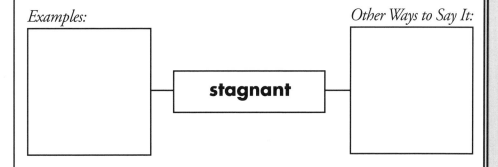

Examples:

stagnant

Other Ways to Say It:

Where might you find **stagnant** water?

A Word a Day

unkempt

adjective

not groomed; not neat or tidy

After a week of camping in the wilderness, everybody looked quite **unkempt**.

Which words mean about the same thing as **unkempt**?

- messy
- orderly
- scruffy
- tangled
- elegant

Is it ever OK with your parents for you to look **unkempt**? When? When won't they allow it?

humdrum

adjective

lacking excitement

synonym: boring

The movie was so **humdrum** that I fell asleep.

Which of the following describe something that is **humdrum**?

- watching paint dry
- going to a swimming party
- listening to a fly buzz
- going horseback riding
- spending a day at an amusement park

What are some activities that you find **humdrum**?

A Word a Day, Intermediate • EMC 2718 • ©2002 by Evan-Moor Corp.

replenish

verb

to refill

After the long race, the runners had to **replenish** the water in their bodies.

Copy and complete this word map for **replenish**:

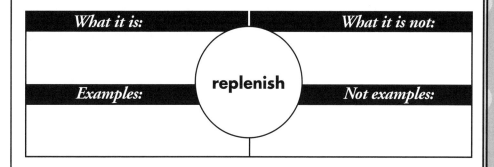

What types of foods do you eat to **replenish** your body with nutrients?

agriculture

noun

the work of farming

Agriculture helps provide the fresh foods we eat.

Which activities would be performed by someone who works in **agriculture**?

- milking cows
- planting seeds
- driving a taxi cab
- driving a tractor
- serving food in a restaurant

Name some of the products of **agriculture** that you eat.

A Word a Day

barricade

1. verb

   to block off

2. noun

   a barrier used to block passage

The fire department had to **barricade** the streets for the parade. They parked their fire trucks across the crosswalks to make a **barricade**.

Copy and complete this Venn diagram for **barricade**:

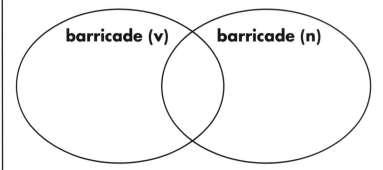

When are **barricades** used to block city streets?

betray

verb

to fail to keep a secret or agreement

Kin Yui didn't mean to **betray** Laura's secret when she told Ana; she thought Ana already knew about it.

Which word or words mean about the same as **betray**?

- guard
- deceive
- protect
- let down
- inform on

Has anyone ever **betrayed** a secret you shared? How did it make you feel? Have you ever **betrayed** a secret anyone has told you? Why?

complement

noun

something that makes something else complete

Cinderella's glass slippers were the perfect **complement** to her gown.

Which of these would **complement** a ball gown?

- high heels
- combat boots
- a flannel shirt
- a diamond necklace
- matching fingernail polish

What types of desserts **complement** your favorite foods?

defiant

adjective

bold in standing up against someone or something

The colonists were **defiant** when the King's soldiers ordered them to return home.

Copy and complete this word map for **defiant**:

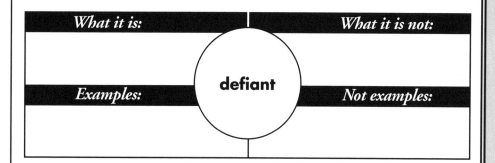

What it is:		What it is not:
	defiant	
Examples:		Not examples:

When is it good to be **defiant**? When is it not such a good idea?

A Word a Day

diligent

adjective

hardworking

Amy is a **diligent** student who always turns in her homework on time.

Which of the following describe a **diligent** worker?

- comes to work early
- takes long lunch breaks
- doesn't care if the job is done on time
- takes lots of long vacations
- works late to get the job done

Describe the study habits of a **diligent** student.

efficient

adjective

doing a job with the least amount of effort or materials and in a timely manner

Pete was such an **efficient** busboy that he could stack and carry all the plates on the table at once.

Which words describe someone who is **efficient**?

- slow
- careful
- capable
- confused
- organized

What do you think is the most **efficient** way to figure out how many students there are in your grade at school?

A Word a Day, Intermediate • EMC 2718 • ©2002 by Evan-Moor Corp.

A Word a Day

outwit

verb

to be more clever than someone else

Edmond could **outwit** any chess player.

Copy and complete this word map for **outwit**:

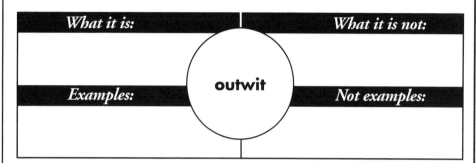

Give examples of situations in which people try to **outwit** each other.

glamorous

adjective

full of charm and elegance

synonym: enchanting

Heads turned as the **glamorous** movie star walked down the red carpet.

Copy and complete this word map for **glamorous**:

Describe someone you think is **glamorous**. What makes that person seem that way?

A Word a Day

hazardous

adjective

dangerous

antonym: safe

A curvy road becomes even more **hazardous** during heavy rainstorms.

Copy and complete this concept map for **hazardous**:

Examples:

hazardous

Other Ways to Say It:

Describe a **hazardous** situation you have seen or know about.

ventriloquist

noun

an entertainer who speaks without moving his or her lips

The **ventriloquist** made it look like his wooden dummy was telling the jokes.

Which words describe a **ventriloquist**?

- talented
- creative
- uninteresting
- entertaining
- unskilled

Try to act like a **ventriloquist**.

A Word a Day, Intermediate • EMC 2718 • ©2002 by Evan-Moor Corp.

ingenious

adjective

clever or skillful

The **ingenious** children made a skateboard using old roller skates and a piece of wood.

Which words mean about the same thing as **ingenious**?

- dim-witted
- bright
- inventive
- slow
- able

Share some examples of **ingenious** ideas that you or someone else has had.

knickknack

noun

a small ornament or trinket

The souvenir shop at the amusement park was full of **knickknacks**.

Which of the following items are **knickknacks**?

- hand-made mittens
- a small porcelain dog
- a fishing rod
- a glass egg
- a ceramic cow

Do you have a **knickknack** that is special to you? Tell your class about it. Are there any **knickknacks** that you like to collect?

A Word a Day

landscape

1. verb

   to make the natural features of an outdoor area more attractive by adding trees or plants

2. noun

   an area of outdoor scenery

After we **landscape** the yard, the **landscape** outside the living room window will be more pleasant.

Copy and complete this Venn diagram for **landscape**:

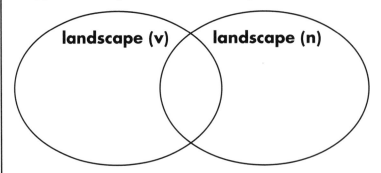

landscape (v)   landscape (n)

What is your favorite type of **landscape**? Do you like the mountains, the desert, or the beach?

lenient

adjective

not strict; mild

Mrs. Johnson was so **lenient** about deadlines that most students turned in their projects late.

Which words mean about the same thing as **lenient**?

- easygoing
- relaxed
- severe
- permissive
- mean

Describe someone you know who is **lenient**.

A Word a Day, Intermediate • EMC 2718 • ©2002 by Evan-Moor Corp.

kowtow

verb

1. to show respect or unquestioning obedience

2. in traditional China, a bow from a kneeling position where the forehead touches the ground as a way to show respect

Our team captain acts like he expects the rest of the team to **kowtow** to him. You'd have to be on the gymnastics team to be flexible enough to **kowtow**!

Which of these people would children **kowtow** to in Ancient China?

- a baby
- their grandfather
- a teacher
- the emperor
- their classmates

Have you ever felt like someone expects you to **kowtow** to him or her? How did you feel about it?

justify

verb

to give a reason for something

Mark knew he could **justify** getting home from school late after explaining that the bus got a flat tire.

Which of these situations could you probably **justify**?

- swatting a fly
- stealing a diamond ring
- returning a library book after the due date
- eating a piece of your sister's Halloween candy
- lying to your teacher

Tell about a time when you avoided getting in trouble because you could **justify** your behavior.

A Word a Day

enthusiasm

noun

a strong feeling of excitement or interest

synonym: eagerness

Stella's **enthusiasm** for the ballet soon had the whole class eager to attend the performance.

Copy and complete this concept map for **enthusiasm**:

Examples:

enthusiasm

Other Ways to Say It:

What makes you feel **enthusiasm**? How do you express it?

establish

verb

to set up

The telephone company decided to **establish** Internet service in large cities before small towns.

Which of these do you do when you **establish** something?

- form something new
- demolish something
- install something new
- create something
- eliminate something

When was the United States of America **established** as an independent nation?

A Word a Day, Intermediate • EMC 2718 • ©2002 by Evan-Moor Corp.

flounder

1. noun

   a flatfish that lives in salt water

2. verb

   to struggle awkwardly

As the fisherman removed the hook from its mouth, the **flounder** began to **flounder** and thrash in the bottom of the rowboat.

Which of these might **flounder** about?

- a cat that falls into a tub full of water
- a runner headed for the finish line
- someone trying to learn to balance on a unicycle
- a ballerina performing onstage
- someone walking through an unfamiliar room in the dark

Name some creatures that might **flounder** about when removed from their natural habitat.

frigid

adjective

very cold

antonym: warm

Though the water in the lake was **frigid** in December, it remained unfrozen.

Which of these would be **frigid**?

- a January morning in New York
- the summit of Mount Everest
- a sand castle
- an iceberg
- a July afternoon in Florida

Have you ever been swimming in **frigid** water? Have you ever been outdoors in **frigid** weather? Tell your class about it.

A Word a Day

narrative

noun

a story or narration

Ms. Sanchez read the class a first-person **narrative** written by a soldier in the Civil War.

Copy and complete this word map for **narrative**:

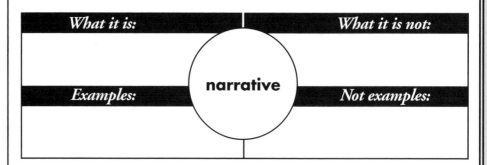

What is a **narrative** that you have enjoyed reading or listening to?

patriot

noun

someone who loves and supports his or her country

Soldiers who give their lives to defend their country are true **patriots**.

Which of these people would you describe as a **patriot**? Why?

- Abraham Lincoln
- Bozo the Clown
- John F. Kennedy
- Susan B. Anthony
- Benedict Arnold

Describe some of the ways that you can show you are a **patriot**.

A Word a Day, Intermediate • EMC 2718 • ©2002 by Evan-Moor Corp.

recommend

verb

to state support of
someone or something

I **recommend** the fresh fish at this
restaurant; it was delicious the last time
we ate here.

Which of these would you **recommend** to a friend?

- A book that you enjoyed.
- A shop that sells overpriced merchandise.
- A Web site with lots of information for a report.
- A beach with dangerous currents.
- A new recording by one of your favorite groups.

What food would you **recommend** at your favorite restaurant?

penetrate

verb

to go into or pass
through something

The attackers could not **penetrate** the stone
walls of the castle.

Which of these would be difficult to **penetrate**?

- a boulder
- mud
- pavement
- an orange
- glass

What would you use to **penetrate** ice?

A Word a Day

rickety

adjective

likely to fall or break due to weakness

synonym: shaky

The **rickety** fence finally fell down during the last storm.

Which of these is most likely to become **rickety**?

- a marble column
- wooden stairs
- a tower made of pick-up sticks
- a tree house built by children
- an iron beam

Give an example of something you've seen that is **rickety**.

scavenger

noun

an animal that eats dead and decaying animals

The deer's carcass was soon picked clean by the **scavengers**.

Which of these animals are **scavengers**?

- hyenas
- cats
- vultures
- rats
- rabbits

Why are **scavengers** an important part of a food web?

A Word a Day, Intermediate • EMC 2718 • ©2002 by Evan-Moor Corp.

trivial

adjective

of little or no importance

The friends decided it was **trivial** to argue over who would pay the bus fare.

Copy and complete this word map for **trivial**:

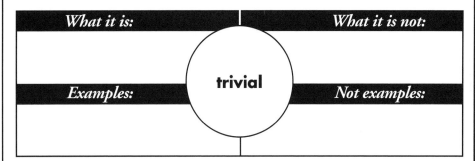

What it is:		What it is not:
	trivial	
Examples:		Not examples:

What types of **trivial** matters have you argued over? Was it worth it?

hemisphere

noun

one half of the earth

The earth can be divided into northern and southern **hemispheres**, or eastern and western **hemispheres**.

In which **hemisphere** is each of these places located?

- Asia
- Antarctica
- South America
- the United States
- Europe

If you could choose to live anywhere on Earth, which **hemisphere** would you choose?

A Word a Day

ambition

noun

a strong desire to achieve a specific goal

Mark's **ambition** was to learn to surf.

Copy and complete this concept map for **ambition**:

Examples:

ambition

Other Ways to Say It:

What do you have the **ambition** to learn or do?

dingy

adjective

having a dirty or dull appearance

After years of hanging in the dusty windows, the white lace curtains looked **dingy**.

Which words mean about the same thing as **dingy**?

- bright
- drab
- clean
- soiled
- discolored

What is something in your classroom or school that looks **dingy**?

A Word a Day, Intermediate • EMC 2718 • ©2002 by Evan-Moor Corp.

transmit

verb

1. to pass from one person or place to another

2. to send out signals by radio or television

When the flu season begins, people try not to **transmit** their germs. Some radio stations even **transmit** information on how to stay healthy.

Copy and complete this Venn diagram for **transmit**:

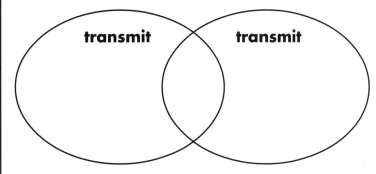

How many ways can you think of to **transmit** a message?

encounter

noun

an unexpected meeting

An **encounter** with a bear was the biggest surprise of our hike.

Which of the following describe an **encounter**?

• Two friends meet at a restaurant for lunch.

• You run into a classmate at the park after school.

• You meet a distant cousin at a family reunion.

• Two strangers bump into each other on the street.

• A group of hikers find a rattlesnake coiled next to the path.

Tell about an **encounter** you had with a classmate outside of school.

A Word a Day

bygone

adjective

anything that is gone or past

synonym: previous

Antique stores are full of things from **bygone** times.

Copy and complete this concept map for **bygone**:

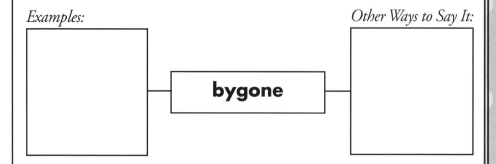

Examples:

Other Ways to Say It:

bygone

Give an example of something from a **bygone** time.

renovate

verb

to make like new

synonym: to restore

The school spent over one million dollars to **renovate** the old gym.

Which of the following can be **renovated**?

- an old house
- an Italian dinner
- a medieval cathedral
- a run-down neighborhood
- a Christmas tree

What structure in your town needs to be **renovated**?

A Word a Day, Intermediate • EMC 2718 • ©2002 by Evan-Moor Corp.

bloat

verb

to swell or puff up

If I eat too much, my stomach will bloat.

Copy and complete this concept map for **bloat**:

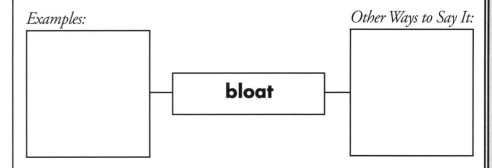

Examples:

bloat

Other Ways to Say It:

Have you ever felt like you were **bloated**? How did it feel?

velocity

noun

a quickness of motion

synonym: speed

A plane travels at a greater velocity than a car.

Which of the following can travel at a high **velocity**?

- a race car
- a horse and buggy
- a speedboat
- a bicycle built for two
- a supersonic jet

Name some things that travel at a low **velocity**.

A Word a Day

dexterity

noun

skill in using the hands

After playing the piano for years, Mei-Ling has wonderful **dexterity**.

Which of the following activities require **dexterity**?

- long-distance running
- playing guitar
- crocheting
- biking
- stringing beads

Tell about something you do that requires **dexterity**.

fickle

adjective

always changing in interests or loyalty

We weren't surprised when Lisa switched teams at the last minute because she is often **fickle**.

Which words mean about the same thing as **fickle**?

- indecisive
- unpredictable
- definite
- changeable
- stable

Describe a time when you or someone you know acted **fickle**.

A Word a Day, Intermediate • EMC 2718 • ©2002 by Evan-Moor Corp.

elevate

verb

to raise or lift up

The mechanic had to **elevate** the car in order to change the flat tire.

Copy and complete this word map for **elevate**:

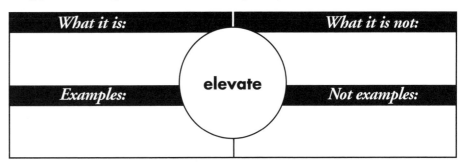

What it is:		What it is not:
Examples:	elevate	Not examples:

What are some reasons that your body temperature might be **elevated**?

garland

noun

a wreath

A beautiful **garland** made of holly decorated our front door.

Which of the following can be used to make a **garland**?

- flowers
- leaves
- glass
- ivy
- rocks

What materials might you use to make a Thanksgiving or Christmas **garland**?

A Word a Day

flammable

adjective

easily set on fire

The rags soaked in gasoline were extremely **flammable**.

Copy and complete this concept map for **flammable**:

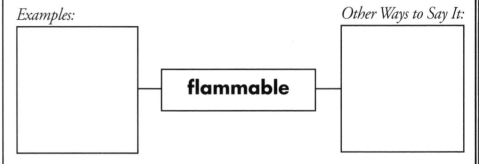

Examples:

flammable

Other Ways to Say It:

Name some other objects that are **flammable**.

horde

noun

a large, moving crowd

synonym: swarm

A **horde** of spectators rushed from the stadium after the powerful earthquake.

Which words mean about the same thing as **horde**?

- group
- couple
- multitude
- trio
- individual

In what type of situation might you see a **horde**?

immaculate

adjective

extremely clean and neat

Molly's mother was pleased to see that her bedroom was **immaculate**.

Copy and complete this concept map for **immaculate**:

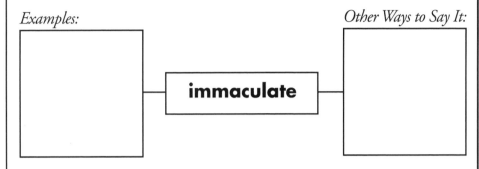

Examples:

immaculate

Other Ways to Say It:

Why is it important for a hospital to be **immaculate**?

junction

noun

a place where things meet or cross

We live at the **junction** of Main and Maple Streets.

Where can you find a **junction**?

- on major roadways
- in the ocean
- on railroad tracks
- on a beach
- in the sky

What is a **junction** near your home?

A Word a Day

yearn

verb

to have a strong wish or longing for something

Margo **yearned** to see her old friends again after she moved to a new school.

Copy and complete this concept map for **yearn**:

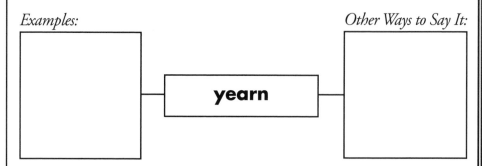

Examples: *Other Ways to Say It:*

yearn

What would you **yearn** for if you couldn't have it anymore?

collate

verb

to put pages together in the correct order

We had to **collate** the pages written by each student to make our class book.

Which of the following would you need to **collate**?

- pages of a picture dictionary that you made
- several copies of a poem
- pages to make a calendar
- pages in a paperback book
- articles written by different people for a school magazine

How would you figure out how to **collate** the pages in a class dictionary?

A Word a Day, Intermediate • EMC 2718 • ©2002 by Evan-Moor Corp.

tuition

noun

money paid for instruction at a school or college

My sister is saving all the money from her paper route for her college **tuition**.

Copy and complete this word map for **tuition**:

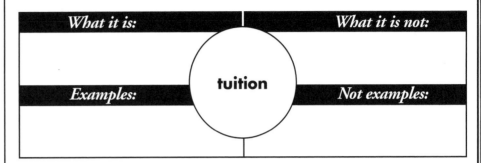

Name some schools that require students to pay **tuition** in order to attend.

tamper

verb

to interfere with something in order to damage or alter it

It is illegal to **tamper** with votes during an election.

Which word or words mean about the same thing as **tamper**?

- mess with
- leave alone
- change
- meddle
- respect

How are medicines and other products packaged to prevent people from **tampering** with them?

A Word a Day

vigorous

adjective

full of strength and energy

We played a **vigorous** game of kickball at recess.

Which of the following activities are **vigorous**?

- running
- fishing
- writing
- aerobics
- dancing

Name some **vigorous** activities that you enjoy.

flourish

verb

to grow or develop in a strong and healthy way

We hope our tomato plants will **flourish** in the rich soil.

Copy and complete this concept map for **flourish**:

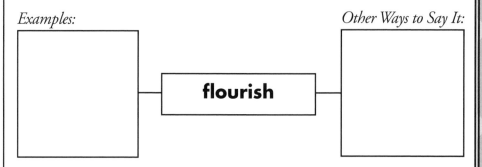

Examples: *Other Ways to Say It:*

flourish

What are some things you can do to help make plants **flourish**?

snob

noun

a person who feels he or she is better than others

Carrie is such a **snob** that she won't ride the bus; she prefers to take a taxi or limousine.

Which of these describe a **snob**?

- expects to be waited on by others
- treats everyone with kindness
- brags about possessions and accomplishments
- is eager to do extra work in a group project
- wants to wear only clothes with designer labels

How would you explain to a **snob** that people are all equal?

congested

adjective

1. to be overcrowded or filled to overflowing
2. having too much mucus in a body part

While we were driving to the pharmacy, an accident caused the street to become **congested** with traffic. While we waited for traffic to get moving, I could hardly breathe because my sinuses were so **congested**.

Copy and complete this Venn diagram for **congested**:

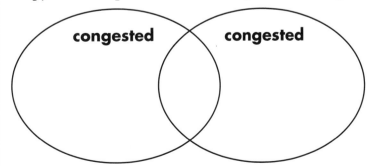

What place in your town gets **congested**?

A Word a Day

blotch

noun

a large spot or stain

The grape juice left a dark **blotch** on the white carpet.

Copy and complete this word map for **blotch**:

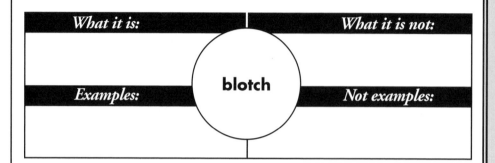

What might you do to hide a **blotch** on a carpet?

automatic

adjective

operating without a person's control

The new coffee maker is completely **automatic**: you just add water and coffee and set the timer, and you have fresh coffee in the morning!

Which of the following items are **automatic**?

- a dishwasher
- a broom
- scissors
- an electric can opener
- motion-sensitive lights

What is something **automatic** that helps you do chores or work?

glutton

noun

someone who eats and drinks with greed

An all-you-can-eat restaurant is the perfect place for a **glutton**.

Copy and complete this concept map for **glutton**:

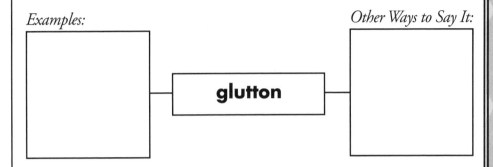

Examples:

glutton

Other Ways to Say It:

Have you ever eaten like a **glutton**? What made you eat that way? How did you feel afterward?

implore

verb

to ask for something with a serious state of mind or a heavy heart

synonym: to beg

It doesn't matter how much we **implore**—our mother never lets us rent PG-13 movies.

Which of the following words mean about the same thing as **implore**?

- command
- plead
- pray
- demand
- request

If you were president, what would you **implore** the people of this nation to do?

A Word a Day

harmonious

adjective

having all parts in agreement

After the argument was settled, a **harmonious** feeling returned to the class.

Which of the following describe something **harmonious**?

- an orchestra playing together
- a heated debate in the halls of Congress
- a lakeshore at sunset, with insects buzzing and birds chirping
- preschool children arguing over toys in a sandbox
- a team of Alaskan huskies pulling a sled over the snow

What can you do to help make your classroom a **harmonious** place?

deplete

verb

to empty

I **depleted** my savings when I bought my new basketball shoes.

Which of the following is it possible to **deplete**?

- underground deposits of oil
- money in a bank account
- water from the ocean
- grain stored in a silo
- tears from your eyes

Name some things at home or school that can be **depleted**.

A Word a Day, Intermediate • EMC 2718 • ©2002 by Evan-Moor Corp.

rendezvous

1. noun

   a place for meeting

2. verb

   to meet at a previously arranged time and place

The playground was a popular **rendezvous** for the girls on the basketball team. They planned to **rendezvous** there right after school.

At which of these locations might a sports team **rendezvous**?

- in a dark alley
- at a pizza parlor
- in the school gymnasium
- at the museum of natural history
- at a stadium

If you had to plan a **rendezvous** in your town, where would it be?

ponder

verb

to think about something very carefully

You should take some time to **ponder** the question before writing your response.

Copy and complete this word map for **ponder**:

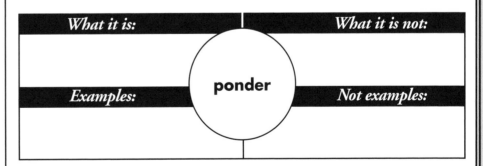

What is something you have had to **ponder**?

A Word a Day

noxious

adjective

harmful to the health of living beings

They evacuated the workers after a **noxious** gas spilled at the factory.

Which words mean about the same thing as **noxious**?

- toxic
- deadly
- helpful
- dangerous
- healthy

Name some products in your home that could be **noxious**.

quagmire

noun

a swampy area

I lost my shoe in the mud when I stepped in the **quagmire**.

Copy and complete this concept map for **quagmire**:

Examples: *Other Ways to Say It:*

Describe what you think a **quagmire** looks, smells, and feels like.

A Word a Day, Intermediate • EMC 2718 • ©2002 by Evan-Moor Corp.

A Word a Day

whimsical

adjective

having the possibility of changing at any time

synonym:
unpredictable

It was difficult to learn the dance routine when our **whimsical** teacher added new moves every week.

Which words mean about the same thing as **whimsical**?

- stable
- variable
- believable
- changeable
- predictable

Describe someone you know who is **whimsical**.

killjoy

noun

a person who spoils the fun of others

Marcy was a **killjoy** when she insisted on telling us the calories in each dish.

Which of these describe a **killjoy**? Someone who:

- says you won't enjoy the movie you're about to see.
- works with you to plan a surprise party for a friend.
- raves about the paintings you'll see at an exhibit.
- lists all the diseases you might catch on your foreign vacation.
- tells you who did it before you finish reading your mystery novel.

How can you help a **killjoy** have a good time, even when that person is sure he or she won't?

A Word a Day

versatile

adjective

able to do many different things well

A **versatile** athlete can run, throw, and kick very well.

Which words mean about the same thing as **versatile**?

- rigid
- flexible
- adaptable
- unchanging
- multitalented

Are you a **versatile** athlete, student, artist, or musician? Describe ways in which you are **versatile**.

convertible

1. noun

   an automobile with a top that can be folded back or removed

2. adjective

   able to be changed

Even with the top down on the **convertible**, we couldn't fit the **convertible** sofa bed into the car.

Copy and complete this Venn diagram for **convertible**:

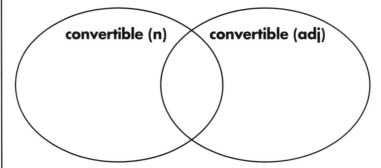

What is something you own, or would like to own, that is **convertible**?

A Word a Day, Intermediate • EMC 2718 • ©2002 by Evan-Moor Corp.

gratify

verb

to please

I usually like to eat dessert after meals to **gratify** my sweet tooth.

Which words mean about the same thing as **gratify**?

- satisfy
- enchant
- annoy
- delight
- irritate

Describe something that **gratifies** you.

impartial

adjective

not favoring one over the other

synonym: fair

It was hard for the referee to be **impartial** when his son's team was playing.

Copy and complete this word map for **impartial**:

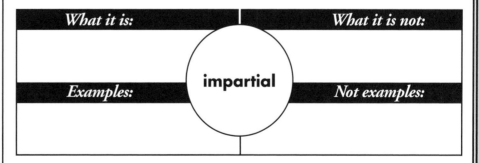

Why do you suppose it's important to have **impartial** judges?

A Word a Day

knoll

noll

noun

a small rounded hill

We can sit on the **knoll** and watch the sun set.

At which of these places might you find a **knoll**?

- in the country
- in the ocean
- on a golf course
- on a tennis court
- on a farm

Where is the **knoll** nearest to your home?

tolerate

tolerate

verb

to be able to put up with something

synonym: to endure

When my dog could no longer **tolerate** the kitten's playful nibbling, he turned around and barked at her.

Copy and complete this word map for **tolerate**:

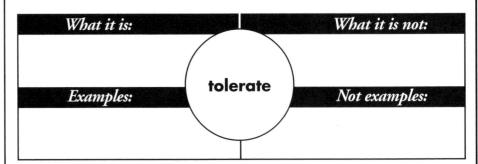

What it is:	*What it is not:*
Examples:	*Not examples:*

tolerate

Give an example of something you cannot **tolerate**.

A Word a Day, Intermediate • EMC 2718 • ©2002 by Evan-Moor Corp.

amateur

adjective

a person who does something for pleasure, not for pay

Many professional golfers first began playing as **amateurs**.

Which words mean about the same thing as **amateur**?

- pro
- expert
- beginner
- unpaid
- instructor

What are some of the positive things about being an **amateur**?

rebellion

noun

a show of opposition to a form of authority

The Minutemen were an important part of the colonial **rebellion** against Britain.

Copy and complete this concept map for **rebellion**:

Examples: *Other Ways to Say It:*

rebellion

What might be some of the reasons for people starting a **rebellion**?

A Word a Day

appease

verb

to give in to demands

synonym: to satisfy

The band came back on stage and played another song to **appease** their fans.

Which word or words mean about the same thing as **appease**?

- please
- calm down
- refuse
- soothe
- reject

Do your parents ever do anything to **appease** you? What are your demands, and how do you hope they will **appease** you?

partial

1. adjective

   not complete

2. verb

   showing unfair favor to one side

My teacher will not accept **partial** homework assignments, even from the students she seems to be **partial** to.

Copy and complete this Venn diagram for **partial**:

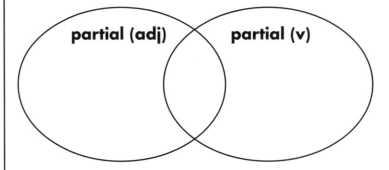

partial (adj)   partial (v)

Can a coach be **partial** to one player over the others? Do you think it's a good idea? Why or why not?

A Word a Day, Intermediate • EMC 2718 • ©2002 by Evan-Moor Corp.

falsehood

noun

an untrue statement

antonym: truth

It was disappointing to learn that the report of a millionaire giving away money was actually a **falsehood**.

Copy and complete this word map for **falsehood**:

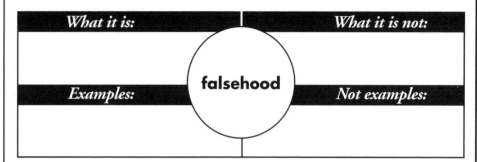

What it is:		What it is not:
	falsehood	
Examples:		Not examples:

Tell of a time when you believed a silly **falsehood**.

navigate

verb

to steer, sail, or direct the course of a ship or aircraft

It was difficult for the skipper to **navigate** the ship in the storm.

Which of the following might help you to **navigate**?

- radar
- a map
- an anchor
- a compass
- a microphone

If you could learn to **navigate**, would you prefer to **navigate** a ship or an airplane? Why?

A Word a Day

kindling

noun

small dried twigs or pieces of wood used to start a fire

The boys had to gather **kindling** before they could build the campfire.

Copy and complete this concept map for **kindling**:

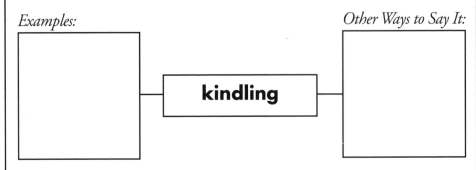

Examples: *Other Ways to Say It:*

kindling

Why do you need **kindling** to start a fire? Where could you find **kindling** near your home?

domestic

adjective

1. related to the home or family
2. tame; not wild

Although I enjoy most **domestic** activities, I hate cleaning up after our **domestic** ferret.

Copy and complete this Venn diagram for **domestic**:

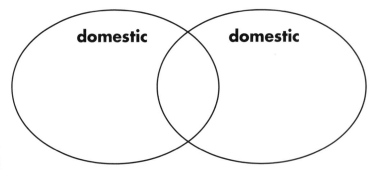

Name some of your **domestic** chores.

A Word a Day, Intermediate • EMC 2718 • ©2002 by Evan-Moor Corp.

rustic

adjective

of the countryside, not the city

The **rustic** cabin looked out of place in the suburban neighborhood.

Copy and complete this concept map for **rustic**:

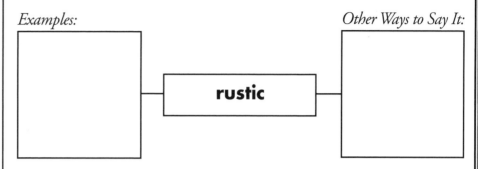

Examples:

rustic

Other Ways to Say It:

What do you like about a **rustic** lifestyle? What do you like about city living?

lapse

1. noun

   something that slips by or passes away

2. verb

   to backslide, or gradually fall into bad habits

In the **lapse** of just one month, he broke his New Year's resolution and began to **lapse** into his old behavior.

Which of the following describe a **lapse**?

- making a promise to always tell the truth
- starting to bite your nails after having quit
- riding a bike to school instead of taking the bus
- typing with two fingers after you've learned to use ten
- eating chocolate two days after deciding to give it up for good

How many months will **lapse** until your next birthday? How many will **lapse** before New Year's is here again?

A Word a Day

correspond

verb

1. to exchange letters with someone

2. to match

When you **correspond** with someone in Japan, you have to write the Japanese pictographs that **correspond** to that person's address.

Which of the following pairs **correspond**?

- the numeral "5" and the word "fifty"
- the numeral "1" and the word "one"
- a red sock and a white sock
- a shoe and a glove
- a jar and its lid

Do you **correspond** with anyone who lives far away? How do you prefer to **correspond**: "snail mail" or e-mail?

coy

adjective

shy or bashful

The **coy** child hid behind her mother when a stranger came to the door.

Copy and complete this word map for **coy**:

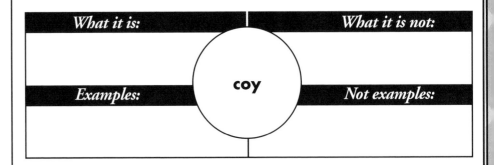

How does a **coy** child act? How is it different from the way a **coy** adult might act?

A Word a Day, Intermediate • EMC 2718 • ©2002 by Evan-Moor Corp.

ancestor

noun

a person from whom you are descended

I have an **ancestor** who fought in the Civil War.

Copy and complete this concept map for **ancestor**:

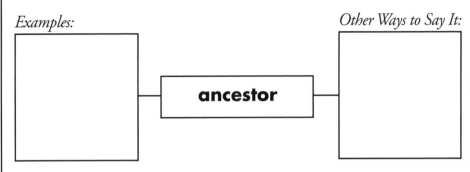

What do you know about your **ancestors**? Who is one of your most interesting **ancestors**?

dimension

noun

a measurement of length, width, or thickness

We need to figure out the room's **dimensions** so we can buy enough paint.

Copy and complete this concept map for **dimension**:

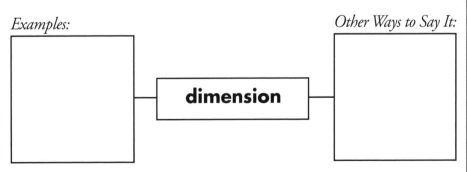

Choose an object in your classroom and guess what its **dimensions** might be. Use a ruler or yardstick to see how close your estimate was to the actual **dimensions**.

A Word a Day

dominate

verb

to rule or control by strength or power

The king used his soldiers to help him **dominate** the kingdom.

Copy and complete this word map for **dominate**:

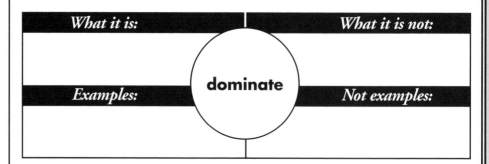

What it is:		*What it is not:*
Examples:	**dominate**	*Not examples:*

Has someone ever tried to **dominate** you? How did you feel? Have you ever tried to **dominate** anyone? Why?

invincible

adjective

not able to be defeated

With five victories and no defeats, our team has been **invincible** this season.

Which of these characters are **invincible**?

- Little Red Riding Hood
- Power Puff Girls
- Little Boy Blue
- Spiderman
- Batman

Do you think there is anyone in real life that is **invincible**? Explain your answer.

A Word a Day, Intermediate • EMC 2718 • ©2002 by Evan-Moor Corp.

muse

verb

to think deeply

My mother had to **muse** for a while before deciding to let me have a slumber party.

Which words mean about the same thing as **muse**?

- meditate
- consider
- ponder
- forget
- ask

What decision have you had to **muse** about? Give an example of something you had to **muse** about recently.

paraphrase

verb

to restate in other words

The teacher asked us to **paraphrase** the story in fifty words or less.

Copy and complete this concept map for **paraphrase**:

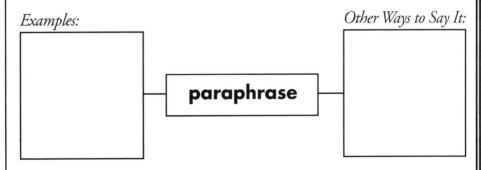

Examples: *Other Ways to Say It:*

paraphrase

Do you prefer to hear someone **paraphrase** an exciting news article, or would you rather hear the whole thing? Why?

A Word a Day

vulnerable

adjective

capable of being harmed or injured

The baby bird was very vulnerable on the ground without its mother.

Which of these animals are **vulnerable**?

- a dog sitting by a warm fireplace
- an orphaned cheetah cub
- a lion alone on the prairie
- a kitten on a busy street
- a dog lost outside

Would you feel **vulnerable** if you had to sleep outdoors without a tent? What other situations might make you feel **vulnerable**?

tariff

noun

a tax paid on products that are imported or exported

Fresh pineapple from Mexico is expensive because of the import tariff.

For which items might you have to pay a **tariff**?

- a German car bought in the United States
- American apples bought in Costa Rica
- a cowboy hat made and sold in Texas
- food from your garden
- a rug made in India

What is something that you or your family has bought that probably included a **tariff**?

A Word a Day, Intermediate • EMC 2718 • ©2002 by Evan-Moor Corp.

urge

1. verb

   to speak or argue strongly for

2. noun

   a strong desire

The basketball coach had to **urge** her star player to control her **urge** to take wild shots.

Copy and complete this Venn diagram for **urge**:

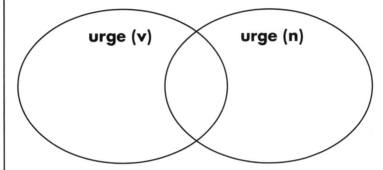

How would you **urge** your family to recycle? What else do you **urge** your family to do?

tactful

adjective

thoughtful and sensitive to others' feelings

The **tactful** waiter quietly removed the glass of water with a fly in it.

Which of these are examples of **tactful** behavior?

- not taking seconds before everyone takes a first serving
- leaving a wet towel on the bathroom floor
- not making noise early in the morning
- tracking mud through the house
- offering to wash the dishes

Give some other examples of **tactful** behavior. What behavior would not be **tactful**?

A Word a Day

belfry

noun

a tower where a bell or bells are hung

The bell ringer climbed the winding staircase to the **belfry** every evening at 5:00.

Which of the following might you see in a **belfry**?

- coins
- stairs
- a bell
- a train
- a rope

Is there a **belfry** in your town? If not, where have you seen a **belfry**?

critique

verb

to give a critical review of something

Before I write my final draft, I will ask my classmates to **critique** my rough draft.

Copy and complete this word map for **critique**:

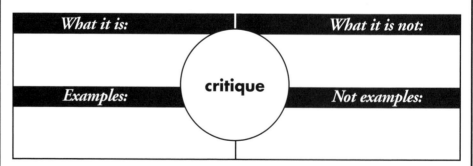

Why might it be difficult to **critique** your own work? Do you think it is easy or difficult to **critique** your best friend's work?

humble

adjective

1. not proud; modest

2. simple; not fancy

The **humble** artist refused to take money for his beautiful paintings. He lived simply in a **humble** studio on the outskirts of the city.

Copy and complete this Venn diagram for **humble**:

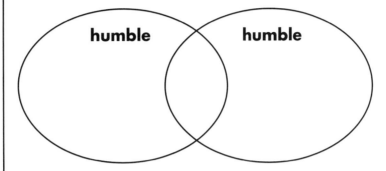

Describe something or someone you know who is **humble**.

friction

noun

a rubbing of one thing against another

The **friction** from swinging on the bars soon raised painful blisters on her hands.

Which of these situations would create **friction**?

- going down a slide
- jumping rope on the playground
- striking a match against a matchbox
- skidding across the pavement on a bike
- swinging next to your friend on a swingset

Describe another way to create **friction**.

A Word a Day

loathe

verb

to dislike greatly

antonym: to adore

I **loathe** running around the track after it rains because I always get covered with mud.

Which words mean about the same thing as **loathe**?

- appreciate
- despise
- admire
- detest
- hate

What is something you **loathe**? Do you ever **loathe** something that is actually good for you? If so, give an example.

sincere

adjective

genuine; true

Cory's **sincere** apology made me feel better.

Copy and complete this word map for **sincere**:

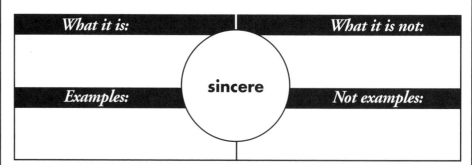

How do you know if someone is being **sincere** or not? How does it feel when someone is not **sincere** with you? Are you always **sincere**?

A Word a Day, Intermediate • EMC 2718 • ©2002 by Evan-Moor Corp.

A Word a Day

tragedy

noun

1. an extremely sad or unfortunate occurrence

2. a play, movie, or story with a terribly sad ending

The sinking of the ocean liner *Titanic* was a terrible **tragedy**. It cost millions of dollars to film the **tragedy** *Titanic*, which was a huge hit.

Copy and complete this Venn diagram for **tragedy**:

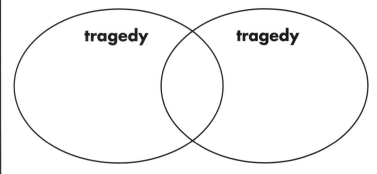

Tell the plot of a **tragedy** that you've read, seen as a play, or seen at the movie theater.

pulsate

verb

to beat or throb in rhythm, as the heart does

On foggy nights, you can see the glow of the roller coaster's flashing neon lights **pulsate** in the sky.

Copy and complete this concept map for **pulsate**:

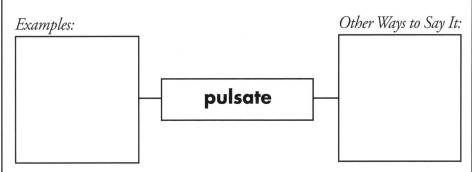

Can you think of a time when your heart was beating so fast that you could feel the blood **pulsate** in your body? Where in your body did you feel it? What had you been doing?

A Word a Day

undaunted

adjective

not discouraged; not hesitating because of fear

The hiker remained **undaunted** even though he had been lost for two days before being rescued.

Which words mean about the same thing as **undaunted**?

- unafraid
- fearless
- terrified
- scared
- brave

Give an example of someone who was **undaunted**. Have you ever been **undaunted**? Describe the situation.

aptitude

noun

a natural ability or talent

Lucita showed a strong **aptitude** for painting.

Copy and complete this word map for **aptitude**:

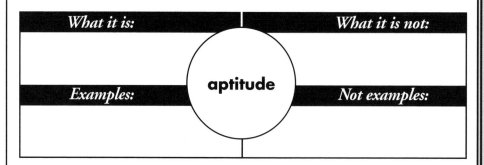

Have you discovered something for which you have an **aptitude**? Tell the class about it.

A Word a Day, Intermediate • EMC 2718 • ©2002 by Evan-Moor Corp.

balmy

adjective

soothing and mild

The **balmy** spring weather felt refreshing after the long winter.

Which words mean about the same thing as **balmy**?

- fair
- cold
- warm
- harsh
- gentle

Describe a **balmy** spring day or a **balmy** tropical night.

bask

verb

to bathe in warm sunlight

As cold-blooded animals, snakes can raise their body temperature by **basking** in the sun.

Copy and complete this concept map for **bask**:

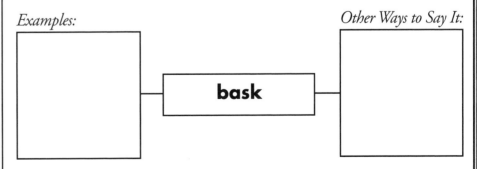

Examples: *Other Ways to Say It:*

bask

What other animals **bask** in the sun? Do you like to **bask** in the sun?

A Word a Day

denominator

noun

the number below the line in a fraction

In a fraction, the **denominator** indicates the number of parts a whole number is divided into.

Which of these fractions is equivalent to one that has a **denominator** of 8 and a numerator of 4?

- ¼
- ¾
- ½
- ³⁄₆
- ⁸⁄₄

If you were dividing a pizza into 10 pieces, what number would be in the **denominator** of the fraction that represents one slice of pizza?

vertical

adjective

straight up and down

The first hill on the roller coaster was almost **vertical**.

Copy and complete this concept map for **vertical**:

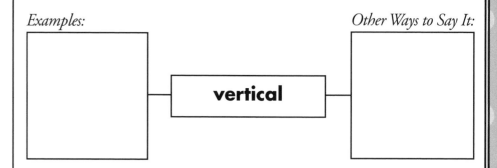

Examples:

vertical

Other Ways to Say It:

Name some things in your classroom that are **vertical**.

ovation

noun

a loud and enthusiastic show of approval

The choir received a standing **ovation** when they finished performing.

In which of these places might you give an **ovation**?

- waiting in line for the restroom
- a skating competition
- a football game
- a piano recital
- a taxi ride

When and where was the last time you gave an **ovation**?

emancipate

verb

to set free from slavery or control

President Lincoln helped to **emancipate** the slaves in the South.

Copy and complete this word map for **emancipate**:

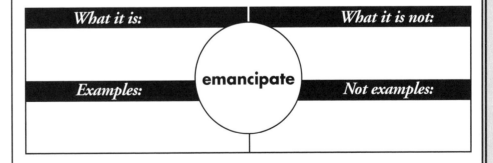

In what other times or places have people struggled to **emancipate** themselves?

A Word a Day

susceptible

adjective

easily influenced or affected

The medical assistant took vitamins so she wouldn't be **susceptible** to catching colds.

Which words mean about the same thing as **susceptible**?

- unprotected
- undefended
- sensitive
- secure
- safe

Are you **susceptible** to poison oak or poison ivy? What is something else you are **susceptible** to?

tarnish

verb

to dull the shine of a metal surface

Silver will **tarnish** if it's not polished or stored in a closed container.

Which of these items could **tarnish**?

- a wooden bowl on a shelf
- a brass tea kettle on the stove
- a glass vase on a wooden table
- a copper picture frame on the mantel
- Grandmother's fine silverware in its velvet case

Is there anything in your classroom that can **tarnish**? What about in your home?

A Word a Day, Intermediate • EMC 2718 • ©2002 by Evan-Moor Corp.

pell-mell

adjective

in confusion and disorder

The books were thrown **pell-mell** onto the shelf.

Which words mean about the same thing as **pell-mell**?

- carelessly
- carefully
- sloppily
- neatly
- hastily

Describe a room in your house or at school where things are thrown about **pell-mell**.

negligent

adjective

not showing proper care or concern

Only a **negligent** pet owner would allow a sick dog to howl in pain all night long.

Copy and complete this word map for **negligent**:

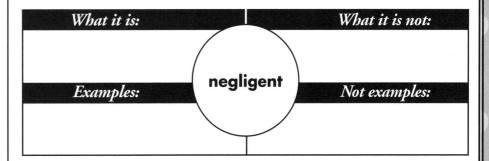

Give an example of **negligent** behavior that you have seen or heard about. Have you ever been **negligent** about anything?

A Word a Day

undeniable

adjective

unquestionably true

After the first snowfall, it was **undeniable** that winter had truly arrived.

Which words mean about the same thing as **undeniable**?

- questionable
- evident
- certain
- obvious
- false

Tell an **undeniable** fact about yourself.

scuffle

noun

a confused struggle or fight

The argument became a **scuffle** when one boy grabbed the other's cap.

Copy and complete this concept map for **scuffle**:

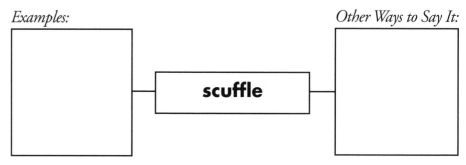

Examples: *Other Ways to Say It:*

scuffle

Where might you see a **scuffle** take place?

A Word a Day, Intermediate • EMC 2718 • ©2002 by Evan-Moor Corp.

tantalize

verb

to tease by showing something and then keeping it out of reach

It is cruel to **tantalize** caged animals with tempting foods.

Which of these edibles could you use to **tantalize** someone?

- a piece of chocolate cake
- a big bowl of ice cream
- a piece of stale bread
- a strawberry sundae
- a charred hot dog

What can **tantalize** you? What could you use to **tantalize** your best friend?

contemporary

adjective

up to date; modern or current

antonym: old

The **contemporary** digital clock looked out of place among the antique furnishings.

Copy and complete this word map for **contemporary**:

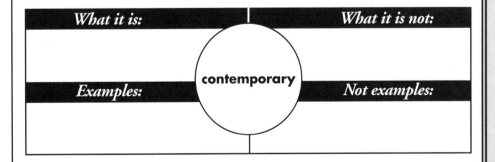

Describe some items in your own home that are **contemporary**.

A Word a Day

vicinity

noun

neighborhood

There are three playgrounds in the **vicinity** of my home.

Which of these things might be in the **vicinity** of where you live?

- the Rocky Mountains
- Disney World
- a post office
- a park
- a school

Tell the class about some of the unusual things in the **vicinity** of your home.

annex

1. verb

   to add or attach to something larger

2. noun

   a wing added to a building

The hospital had to **annex** the neighboring building when it opened the new pediatric **annex**.

Copy and complete this Venn diagram for **annex**:

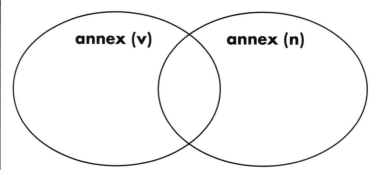

If you could add an **annex** to your home, what would you use it for?

A Word a Day, Intermediate • EMC 2718 • ©2002 by Evan-Moor Corp.

brawny

adjective

muscular and strong

synonym: powerful

The **brawny** lumberjack easily sawed through the logs.

Which words mean about the same thing as **brawny**?

- great
- timid
- mighty
- tough
- weak

Describe someone you know who is **brawny**.

curfew

noun

a deadline for people to be off the streets in the evening

Our community has an eleven o'clock **curfew** for people under sixteen.

Which of these would have the authority to set a **curfew** for you?

- the city government
- your parents
- your teacher
- the president
- your friend

Do you think it is a good idea to have a **curfew** for teenagers? Explain your thinking.

A Word a Day

radiate

verb

to give off rays of heat or light

The heat that **radiated** from the campfire almost melted the soles of my sneakers.

Copy and complete this word map for **radiate**:

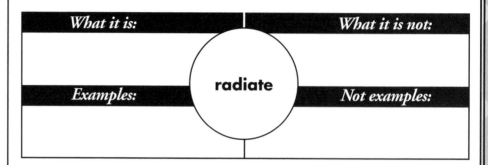

Name some objects that **radiate** light. Name some that **radiate** heat.

prosperous

adjective

having economic well-being

synonym: wealthy

The **prosperous** business donated thousands of dollars to the community.

Which words mean about the same thing as **prosperous**?

- impoverished
- successful
- affluent
- broke
- well-off

How would you live if you were **prosperous**?

A Word a Day, Intermediate • EMC 2718 • ©2002 by Evan-Moor Corp.

endurance

noun

the power to withstand stress or hardship

The marathon runner has the **endurance** to run for thirty miles.

Copy and complete this concept map for **endurance**:

Examples:

endurance

Other Ways to Say It:

Describe someone you know who has amazing **endurance**.

inundate

verb

1. to flood or overflow
2. to overrun or overwhelm

The heavy rains caused the river to rise and **inundate** the lowlands. The nearby fields were **inundated** with ants fleeing from the rising water.

Which of the following could **inundate** an area?

- a swarm of locusts
- a grain of sand
- a hot lava flow
- a mud puddle
- a tidal wave

If your home was going to be **inundated**, what would you grab before leaving?

A Word a Day

vital

adjective

necessary for supporting life

antonym: unimportant

Clean air is **vital** to human survival.

Which of the following are **vital** to survival?

- running shoes
- clean water
- computers
- clothing
- food

What are three things that are **vital** in your life?

phenomenon

noun

1. a fact or an event that can be observed or experienced
2. an extraordinary person or thing

Lightning is a natural **phenomenon** that has always awed people.
The Beatles were a **phenomenon** that thrilled young people during the '60s.

Copy and complete this Venn diagram for **phenomenon**:

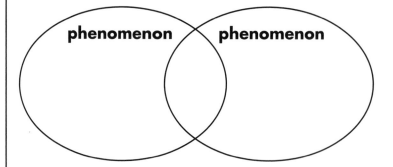

phenomenon   **phenomenon**

Give an example of someone or something that you think is a **phenomenon**.

A Word a Day, Intermediate • EMC 2718 • ©2002 by Evan-Moor Corp.

jostled

verb

bumped or pushed
around roughly

The passengers were **jostled** about when the
train came to a sudden stop.

At which of these places might you get **jostled**?

- at a crowded arena
- playing football
- on a roller coaster
- at a bookstore
- playing golf

Describe a situation in which you were **jostled**.

hearty

adjective

full of warmth and
friendliness

My grandfather gave us a **hearty** welcome
when we arrived.

Which words mean about the same thing as **hearty**?

- enthusiastic
- cheerful
- tearful
- pitiful
- cold

Who would you greet with a **hearty** welcome? Who welcomes
you with a **hearty** greeting?

A Word a Day

emotion

noun

any strong feeling

The new father was overcome with **emotion** as he gazed at his infant daughter.

Copy and complete this concept map for **emotion**:

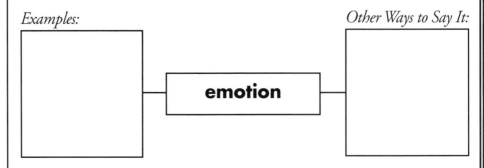

Examples:

emotion

Other Ways to Say It:

What is a difficult **emotion** for you to control? What is your favorite **emotion**? Explain your answers.

procrastinate

verb

to put off doing something until a future time

I can not **procrastinate** any longer because the report is due tomorrow.

Copy and complete this word map for **procrastinate**:

What it is:

What it is not:

procrastinate

Examples:

Not examples:

Do you think it is a good idea to **procrastinate**? Why or why not?

A Word a Day, Intermediate • EMC 2718 • ©2002 by Evan-Moor Corp.

indication

noun

something that points out or indicates

The smiling faces were a good **indication** that everyone was having a good time.

Copy and complete this concept map for **indication**:

Examples: *Other Ways to Say It:*

indication

How can your actions give an **indication** of what your feelings are?

taffeta

noun

a stiff, shiny fabric made of silk, nylon, or acetate

The ballerina's tutu was made of beautiful lavender **taffeta**.

Which of these might be made of **taffeta**?

- a newborn's nightgown
- a military uniform
- an evening gown
- a wedding gown
- a hunting jacket

If you could have something made of **taffeta**, what would it be and what color would it be?

A Word a Day

contribute

verb

1. to give assistance or money
2. to help bring about

The community was able to **contribute** ten thousand dollars for restoring the old schoolhouse. The hard work of many volunteers **contributed** to the successful restoration.

Copy and complete this Venn diagram for **contribute**:

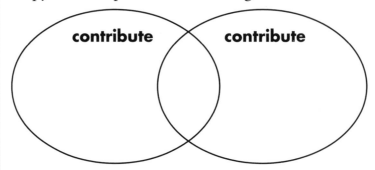

What are some charities that you would like to **contribute** to?

humorous

adjective

full of humor; amusing

synonym: funny

People laughed all evening as they enjoyed the **humorous** play.

Which words mean about the same thing as **humorous**?

- hilarious
- comical
- tragic
- scary
- sad

What is your favorite **humorous** movie?

A Word a Day, Intermediate • EMC 2718 • ©2002 by Evan-Moor Corp.

antidote

noun

something that works against the effects of poison

My snakebite kit includes an **antidote** for venom.

Copy and complete this concept map for **antidote**:

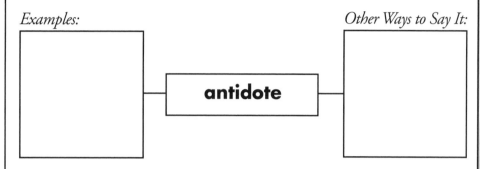

Examples:

antidote

Other Ways to Say It:

Have you ever heard of anyone who had to take an **antidote**? If so, what was it for? What kinds of **antidotes** do you know about?

loiter

verb

to spend time standing about, doing nothing in particular

The shopping center is locked up at night so nobody can **loiter** around the stores.

Which word or words mean about the same thing as **loiter**?

- pass through
- hang around
- move along
- linger
- loaf

What places in your town have rules about **loitering**? Do you think rules against **loitering** are a good idea?

A Word a Day

tattered

adjective

broken down or
worn out

After years of use, the **tattered** leather sofa was finally replaced.

Copy and complete this word map for **tattered**:

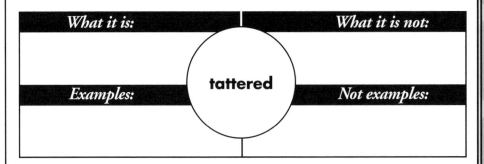

Describe something you have that is **tattered**. Do you throw out **tattered** things, or do you keep them? Do you repair them, or leave them **tattered**?

exquisite

adjective

having an intricate and
beautiful design

The **exquisite** embroidery must have taken hours to complete.

Which words mean about the same thing as **exquisite**?

- valueless

- delicate

- detailed

- crude

- fine

What is something **exquisite** that you have seen? Describe it.

spartan

adjective

characterized by strict self-discipline

The wrestler followed a **spartan** routine in his training.

Which words mean about the same thing as **spartan**?

- self-restrained
- delicate
- severe
- stern
- weak

Could you follow a **spartan** training routine? Do you think having discipline is a good idea? Why or why not?

recoil

verb

to draw back

We saw the dog **recoil** as it came across a rattlesnake in the path.

Copy and complete this word map for **recoil**:

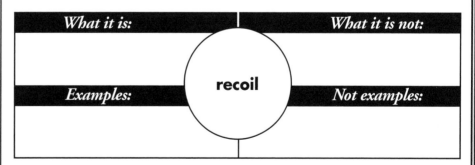

What it is:		*What it is not:*
Examples:	recoil	*Not examples:*

What is something that would make you **recoil**?

A Word a Day

abominable

adjective

something hideous and unappealing

synonym: disgusting

The **abominable** odor nearly knocked me out!

Which words mean about the same thing as **abominable**?

- despicable
- pleasant
- offensive
- lovely
- nasty

Give an example of something you consider **abominable**.

native

noun

a person born in a particular country or place

My grandmother is a **native** of the Philippines.

Which words mean about the same thing as **native**?

- foreigner
- national
- citizen
- local
- alien

Is there anyone in your family who is a **native** of another country? Which one?

A Word a Day, Intermediate • EMC 2718 • ©2002 by Evan-Moor Corp.

disheveled

adjective

untidy; rumpled

After the pillow fight, my bed was totally **disheveled**.

Which words mean about the same thing as **disheveled**?

- disarrayed
- disorderly
- organized
- untidy
- clean

Do you know someone who always looks **disheveled**? Do you ever look **disheveled**? When?

pandemonium

noun

a wild uproar

The stadium burst into **pandemonium** when the home team won the game.

Copy and complete this concept map for **pandemonium**:

Examples:

pandemonium

Other Ways to Say It:

Where might you see **pandemonium** occur?

A Word a Day

terminate

verb

to bring to an end

We had to **terminate** our bike ride when the rain started.

Which words mean about the same thing as **terminate**?

- conclude
- complete
- begin
- finish
- start

If you could choose to **terminate** something, what would it be?

pungent

adjective

sharp or strong to the taste or smell

The **pungent** odor of fish could be smelled all over the wharf.

Copy and complete this word map for **pungent**:

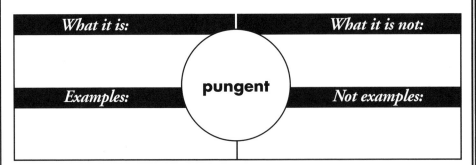

What it is:		*What it is not:*
	pungent	
Examples:		*Not examples:*

Name some other things that can be **pungent**.

pedigree

noun

a list of ancestors of a person or an animal

synonym: descent

Our puppy was expensive because his **pedigree** includes several champion show dogs.

Which word or words mean about the same thing as **pedigree**?

- descendants
- offspring
- family tree
- degree
- lineage

Do you think it's better to have a pet with a **pedigree**? Explain your answer.

condemn

verb

to strongly disapprove of

Our school **condemns** all bullying behavior.

Copy and complete this concept map for **condemn**:

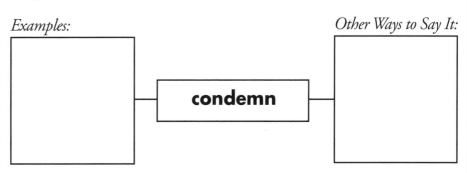

Examples: *Other Ways to Say It:*

condemn

Give an example of something you would **condemn**. Give some examples of actions your school **condemns**.

A Word a Day

chronic

adjective

1. lasting a long time; occurring repeatedly
2. done by habit

My grandma has **chronic** arthritis pain. Instead of being a **chronic** complainer, she uses pain medication.

Which of the following are **chronic** conditions?

- a cold
- asthma
- allergies
- sneezing
- poison oak

Do you have a **chronic** worry about anything? Does anyone else that you know? What causes the worry?

leisure

noun

free time for resting

I enjoy painting during my **leisure** time.

Which word or words mean about the same thing as **leisure**?

- business hours
- school hours
- spare time
- recreation
- relaxation

What do you like to do during your **leisure** time?

A Word a Day, Intermediate • EMC 2718 • ©2002 by Evan-Moor Corp.

retaliate

verb

to get revenge

You can get hurt if you try to **retaliate** against a bully.

Copy and complete this word map for **retaliate**:

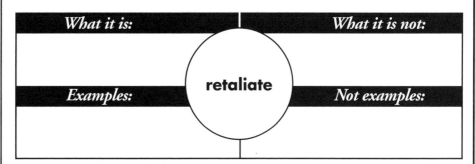

Do you think it's ever a good idea to **retaliate**? Explain your thinking.

translucent

adjective

allowing some light to pass through

antonym: opaque

We could see the sky grow overcast through the **translucent** stained glass windows.

Which of these materials could be **translucent**?

- plastic
- wood
- paper
- glass
- iron

Point out something **translucent** in your classroom or school.

A Word a Day

jut

verb

to stick out

The rocks **jut** out of the water all along the coast.

Copy and complete this concept map for **jut**:

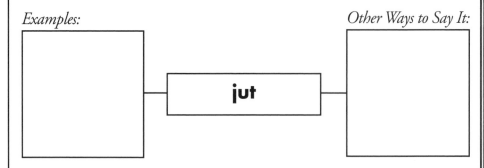

Examples:

Other Ways to Say It:

jut

Describe a geographical feature in your area that **juts** into space or into the water.

asset

noun

something valuable or useful

Her great endurance was a wonderful **asset** to the track team.

Which of these could be an **asset**?

- strength
- selfishness
- a bad temper
- lots of money
- a good memory

What is an **asset** that you or someone else brings to the class or community?

A Word a Day, Intermediate • EMC 2718 • ©2002 by Evan-Moor Corp.

A Word a Day

immerse

verb

1. to cover completely with water or liquid
2. to involve or occupy completely

After the storm, the parking lot was **immersed** in water. She was so **immersed** in her work that she didn't even notice the flood!

Copy and complete this Venn diagram for **immerse**:

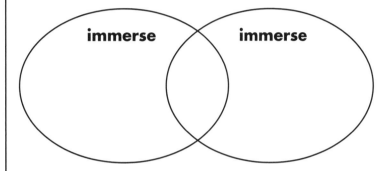

What is something that you like to **immerse** yourself in?

temptation

noun

something that tempts or attracts

It was so hot that I could not fight the **temptation** to jump into the cool water.

Which of these might be a **temptation** for you?

- a spoonful of medicine
- a cold glass of soda
- a chocolate sundae
- a piece of pizza
- liver and onions

What is a **temptation** that you can't resist?

A Word a Day

ravenous

adjective

very hungry

The **ravenous** kittens all fought for a place at the saucer of milk.

Which words mean about the same thing as **ravenous**?

- full
- raving
- starved
- famished
- disinterested

What do you like to eat when you are feeling **ravenous**?

facilitate

verb

to make something easy

The outdoor drop box **facilitates** the return of library materials.

Copy and complete this concept map for **facilitate**:

Examples: *Other Ways to Say It:*

What is something that **facilitates** work at home? What **facilitates** work at school?

condensation

noun

gas or vapor that changes to liquid

After he took a hot shower, the steam in the bathroom created **condensation** on the ceiling.

Which of these are formed by **condensation**?

- rainbows
- clouds
- wind
- mud
- fog

Where have you seen **condensation**?

dormant

adjective

not active; sleeping

The volcano has been **dormant** for hundreds of years.

Copy and complete this concept map for **dormant**:

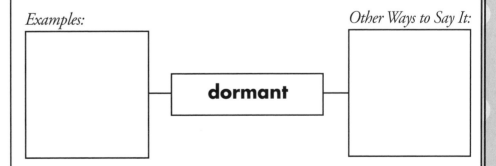

Examples:

dormant

Other Ways to Say It:

What other things in nature can be **dormant**? Name some plants or animals that can be **dormant**.

A Word a Day

remote

adjective

1. far away
2. small, slight

The cabin was in a **remote** location, about 25 miles from the nearest town. There was a **remote** chance that visitors would drop by.

Copy and complete this Venn diagram for **remote**:

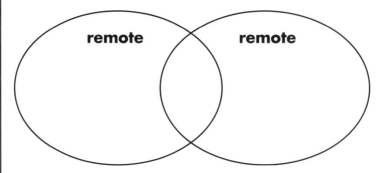

Name some places you know of that are in a **remote** location.

extravagant

adjective

spending lots of money in a free and careless way

He treated his friends to **extravagant** gifts after winning the jackpot.

Which words mean about the same thing as **extravagant**?

- excessive
- wasteful
- lavish
- stingy
- thrifty

What is something **extravagant** that you would buy if you had extra money?

A Word a Day, Intermediate • EMC 2718 • ©2002 by Evan-Moor Corp.

tousled

adjective

in a tangled mass

Her hair was **tousled** after riding in the convertible.

Copy and complete this concept map for **tousled**:

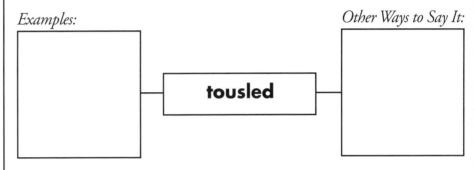

Examples:

tousled

Other Ways to Say It:

When does your hair get **tousled**? What do you do to make it look neat again?

perceive

verb

to become aware of something by experiencing it through the senses

We could barely **perceive** the bird's song over the roar of the waterfall.

Which of the following could you **perceive**?

- people in another country speaking
- images on a movie screen
- roots growing underground
- the smell of burned toast
- a baby crying in her crib

Is it easier for you to **perceive** things that you see or things that you hear?

A Word a Day

overwhelmed

verb

1. to overpower or make helpless

2. to cover or bury completely

The sailors were **overwhelmed** by the force of the storm. Suddenly, the boat was **overwhelmed** by a massive wave.

Copy and complete this Venn diagram for **overwhelmed**:

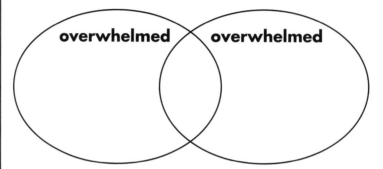

Have you ever felt **overwhelmed**? What was happening? What did you do to feel like you were back in control?

fluctuate

verb

to shift back and forth uncertainly

The weather seemed to **fluctuate** daily, making it hard to schedule the beach party.

Which word or words mean about the same thing as **fluctuate**?

- undergo change
- keep constant
- remain stable
- waver
- vary

What else can **fluctuate** besides the weather?

A Word a Day, Intermediate • EMC 2718 • ©2002 by Evan-Moor Corp.

artifact

noun

an object of interest made in the past by humans

The museum was filled with **artifacts** from early civilizations.

Which of these could be an **artifact**?

- a gold coin
- a new shoe
- a gum wrapper
- an ancient vase
- a Roman mosaic

What sort of **artifact** would you like to see or own?

congenial

adjective

pleasant

The tour guide was very knowledgeable and **congenial**.

Copy and complete this word map for **congenial**:

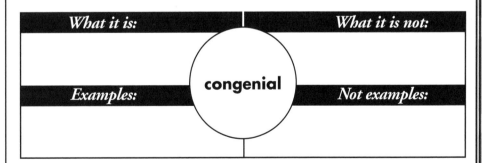

What it is:		*What it is not:*
	congenial	
Examples:		*Not examples:*

Give an example of someone you know who is **congenial**.

A Word a Day

mutter

verb

to speak in a low, unclear way while barely moving the lips

We lose points on our oral reports if we **mutter** when we speak.

Which words mean about the same as **mutter**?

- mumble
- murmur
- whisper
- scream
- shout

Mutter something to your neighbor. Now say it again clearly.

metamorphosis

noun

a complete change in form or appearance

After its **metamorphosis**, a caterpillar becomes a butterfly.

Which words mean about the same thing as **metamorphosis**?

- change
- stability
- endurance
- consistency
- transformation

Describe another animal that experiences **metamorphosis**.

A Word a Day, Intermediate • EMC 2718 • ©2002 by Evan-Moor Corp.

tumultuous

adjective

full of upheaval; wild and chaotic

There was a **tumultuous** sea battle between the pirate ships.

Copy and complete this concept map for **tumultuous**:

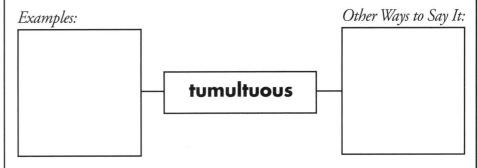

Examples:

Other Ways to Say It:

tumultuous

Give an example of a **tumultuous** period in history.

query

1. noun

   a question

2. verb

   to express doubt about something

The teacher wrote a **query** in the margin of my paper. She **queried** me about the dates I had included.

Copy and complete this Venn diagram for **query**:

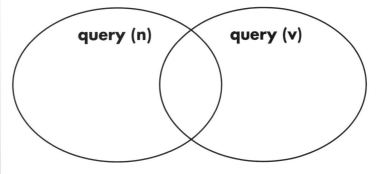

query (n)   query (v)

Give an example of a **query** you need answered.

A Word a Day

diagnosis

noun

a medical opinion given after studying the symptoms

According to the doctor's **diagnosis**, my injured ankle would heal in three months.

Copy and complete this word map for **diagnosis**:

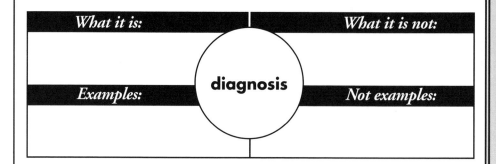

What types of symptoms and procedures would lead to the **diagnosis** of a broken ankle?

jaunty

adjective

stylish

The **jaunty** new sports car costs much more than we can afford.

Copy and complete this concept map for **jaunty**:

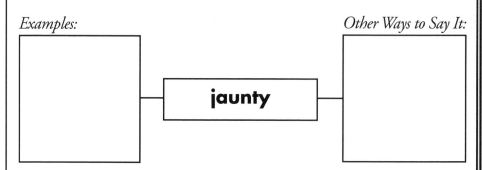

Give an example of something **jaunty** that you would like to own.

A Word a Day, Intermediate • EMC 2718 • ©2002 by Evan-Moor Corp.

wriggle

verb

to squirm

The snake appeared to **wriggle** out of its old skin as he worked to shed it.

Which word or words mean about the same thing as **wriggle**?

- twist
- twitch
- wiggle
- sit still
- stay in place

What is something that makes you **wriggle** and squirm?

corruption

noun

a departure from what is pure or correct

The lawyer was accused of **corruption** after he accepted a bribe.

Copy and complete this word map for **corruption**:

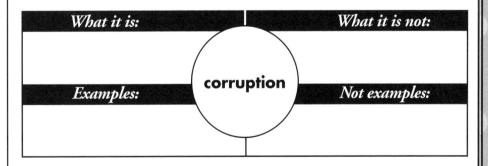

What it is:		What it is not:
	corruption	
Examples:		Not examples:

Who is involved with fighting **corruption**?

A Word a Day

uncouth

adjective

awkward in appearance or behavior

The **uncouth** mountain man stuck out like a sore thumb at the grand ball.

Copy and complete this concept map for **uncouth**:

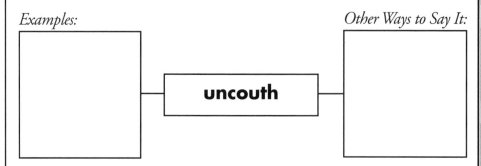

Examples:

Other Ways to Say It:

uncouth

In what type of setting would it be inappropriate to behave in an **uncouth** manner?

aspire

verb

to want or try very hard to achieve a goal

When I grow up, I **aspire** to become a doctor.

Which of these might people **aspire** to become?

- an actor or actress
- a college graduate
- a criminal
- a parent
- an infant

What is something that you **aspire** to?

A Word a Day, Intermediate • EMC 2718 • ©2002 by Evan-Moor Corp.

timber

noun

wood used in building things

synonym: lumber

The **timber** used to build our house came from Pennsylvania.

Copy and complete this word map for **timber**:

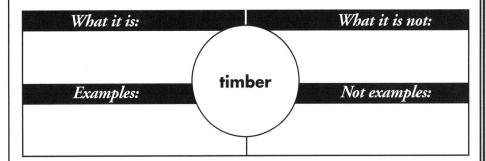

Give some examples of things that are made from **timber**.

mundane

adjective

practical or ordinary

After my ski vacation, a weekend at home seemed very **mundane**.

Which words mean about the same thing as **mundane**?

- exceptional
- everyday
- normal
- special
- usual

What is a **mundane** weekend like for you?

A Word a Day

compile

verb

to put together in a list or volume

We had to **compile** all our stories into a class reader.

Copy and complete this concept map for **compile**:

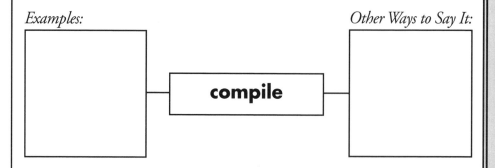

Examples: *Other Ways to Say It:*

compile

What kind of list could you **compile** to help yourself be more organized?

quintessential

adjective

the most typical example of something

The Egyptian pyramids are **quintessential** examples of geometry in architecture.

Which words mean about the same thing as **quintessential**?

- fundamental
- essential
- unusual
- primary
- atypical

What do you think is the **quintessential** characteristic of a successful person?

petty

adjective

not important

It seemed **petty** to argue over who would pay the extra thirty cents.

Copy and complete this word map for **petty**:

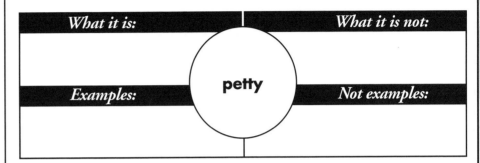

What are some other things that you think are too **petty** to argue about?

venture

noun

a risky undertaking

The business **venture** turned out to be a financial disaster.

Which of these is a **venture**?

- a guaranteed success
- a bet
- an adventure
- a sure thing
- a chance

Give an example of a **venture** you would like to be involved in.

A Word a Day

whim

noun

a sudden idea to do something

I decided to go roller-skating on a **whim**.

Copy and complete this concept map for **whim**:

Examples:

Other Ways to Say It:

whim

List some things you sometimes do on a **whim**.

quizzical

adjective

odd or comical

The actor looked **quizzical** with his face makeup and wild wig.

Which of the following might look **quizzical**?

- a comedian
- a monster
- a puppy
- a clown
- a fly

Can you make a **quizzical** expression on your face? Try it.

A Word a Day

moderate

adjective

not too much or too little

A **moderate** amount of exercise is good for everyone.

Which word or words mean about the same thing as **moderate**?

- a large amount
- a fair amount
- in the middle
- excessive
- average

Give an example of something you do in **moderate** amounts.

fiasco

noun

a complete failure

The pool party was a **fiasco** due to the lightning storm.

Copy and complete this word map for **fiasco**:

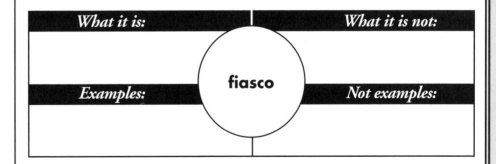

Give examples of something you tried that turned into a **fiasco**.

A Word a Day

gritty

adjective

feeling like sand

After the dentist drilled my tooth, I felt something **gritty** in my mouth.

Which words mean about the same thing as **gritty**?

- wet
- rough
- sandy
- smooth
- scratchy

Where might you expect to step on a **gritty** surface?

contemplate

verb

to think about for a long time

Jeremy took some time to **contemplate** the question before he answered it.

Copy and complete this concept map for **contemplate**:

Examples: *Other Ways to Say It:*

contemplate

What types of decisions cause you to **contemplate**?

A Word a Day, Intermediate • EMC 2718 • ©2002 by Evan-Moor Corp.

diplomatic

adjective

skillful at dealing with people

My teacher is so **diplomatic** at giving feedback that I never get my feelings hurt when she corrects me.

Which of the following people need to be **diplomatic**?

- a political leader
- a mechanic
- an attorney
- a principal
- a baby

Describe someone you know who is **diplomatic**.

taunt

verb

to tease or make fun of

synonym: to mock

It's not a good idea to **taunt** a wild animal.

Which words mean about the same thing as **taunt**?

- jeer
- help
- sneer
- praise
- ridicule

How would you deal with someone who is **taunting** you?

A Word a Day

jester

noun

an entertainer at a royal court in the Middle Ages

The **jester** skipped about happily telling jokes and making people laugh.

Which modern-day entertainers are similar to **jesters**?

- comedians
- rock stars
- acrobats
- singers
- clowns

Who do you think would make a good **jester**?

obsolete

adjective

no longer in use

DVDs may one day make videocassettes **obsolete**.

Copy and complete this word map for **obsolete**:

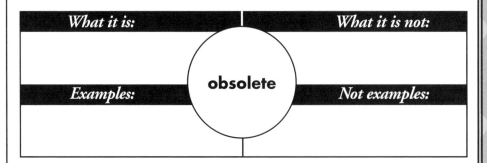

What it is:		*What it is not:*
	obsolete	
Examples:		*Not examples:*

What kind of technology helped make record players **obsolete**? Name some other items that have become **obsolete**. If you can, mention why they became **obsolete**.

A Word a Day, Intermediate • EMC 2718 • ©2002 by Evan-Moor Corp.

exaggerate

verb

to make something seem grander than it actually is

Tall tales usually **exaggerate** certain details to make them more humorous.

Copy and complete this concept map for **exaggerate**:

Examples: *Other Ways to Say It:*

exaggerate

Tell about a time when you **exaggerated** to make something more interesting or humorous.

tendency

noun

a likelihood of behaving in a certain way

A puppy has a **tendency** to chew on things.

Which of these describe a **tendency**?

- a pattern of doing something
- a predictable behavior
- an unexpected event
- a complete surprise
- a sure bet

What do you have a **tendency** to do?

A Word a Day

persistent

adjective

1. not giving up
2. lasting a long time

The **persistent** hikers finally overcame the last obstacle and reached the summit. Their exposure to the cold and frostbite left them with **persistent** circulation problems.

Copy and complete this Venn diagram for **persistent**:

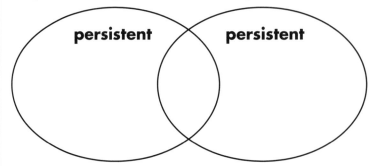

When is it a good idea to be **persistent**? When might it be more effective to be flexible than **persistent**?

extricate

verb

to set free from a difficult or embarrassing situation

antonym: to trap

The bear struggled to **extricate** itself from the net.

Which of these actions might you perform in order to **extricate** something?

- untie
- unlock
- capture
- release
- enclose

Describe a time when you had to **extricate** yourself or someone else from an uncomfortable situation. Where were you, and how did you **extricate** yourself?

A Word a Day, Intermediate • EMC 2718 • ©2002 by Evan-Moor Corp.

frontier

noun

1. the part of a country where people are just beginning to settle
2. the area in a field of study where new discoveries are being made

After the completion of the railroad, many people traveled to the Western **frontier**. Human cloning is one of the **frontiers** of modern science.

Copy and complete this Venn diagram for **frontier**:

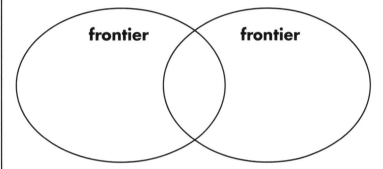

What do you think some new **frontiers** in science may be in the twenty-first century?

flaunt

verb

to display in order to be noticed

The model loved to **flaunt** her expensive clothes.

Which word or words mean about the same thing as **flaunt**?

- parade around
- show off
- cover up
- exhibit
- hide

Tell about something you like to **flaunt**.

A Word a Day

terminology

noun

words or terms used
in a particular business,
science, or art

Doctors learn medical **terminology** as part
of their training.

Copy and complete this word map for **terminology**:

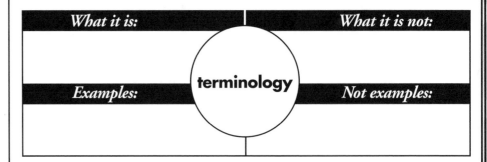

What is some computer **terminology** that you have learned?

digit

noun

1. a numeral
2. a finger

How many **digits** are in the number one
million? Do you have enough **digits** to
represent all those zeros?

Copy and complete this Venn diagram for **digit**:

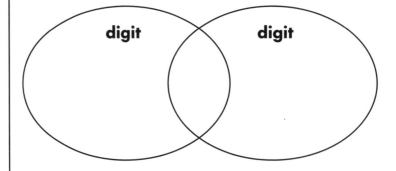

Which animals have **digits** similar to a human's?

A Word a Day, Intermediate • EMC 2718 • ©2002 by Evan-Moor Corp.

perennial

adjective

lasting through the year or for many years

synonym: constant

The **perennial** flowers are sure to bloom again next year.

Which words mean about the same thing as **perennial**?

- seasonal
- temporary
- everlasting
- year-round
- permanent

What kinds of plants are **perennial**?

comprehend

verb

to understand

A good teacher can help you **comprehend** even difficult math problems.

Copy and complete this word map for **comprehend**:

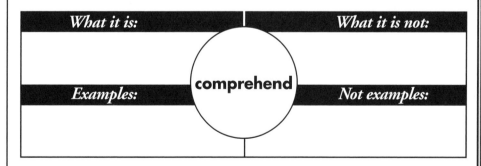

What it is:	What it is not:
Examples: comprehend	Not examples:

Which subjects were once hard for you to understand, but now are easy to **comprehend**?

A Word a Day

deception

noun

a trick or lie meant to deceive someone

antonym: truthfulness

We asked Kari to walk the dog as a **deception** so we could prepare her surprise party.

Which words mean about the same thing as **deception**?

- dishonesty
- honesty
- hoax
- fraud
- truth

Tell about a time when you used **deception** to get what you wanted. Do you think using **deception** is a good idea?

immobile

adjective

unable to move

synonym: motionless

A car is totally **immobile** without its battery.

Copy and complete this concept map for **immobile**:

Examples:

Other Ways to Say It:

immobile

How would you feel if you had to remain completely **immobile** for a long time?

A Word a Day, Intermediate • EMC 2718 • ©2002 by Evan-Moor Corp.

avert

verb

1. to turn away from
2. to prevent

The sun was so bright that I had to **avert** my eyes. I was able to **avert** an accident by avoiding the branch in the road.

Copy and complete this Venn diagram for **avert**:

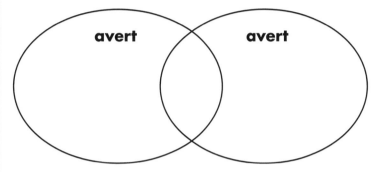

Do you participate in any activities in which you need to be careful to **avert** serious injuries?

majority

noun

more than half

The **majority** of the students in my class ride a bus to school.

Which of these mean about the same thing as **majority**?

- the greater number
- the most popular
- the largest part
- only a few
- a little bit

What does the **majority** of your class like to do at recess?

A Word a Day

fastidious

adjective

not easy to please

The **fastidious** eater complained about every dish served at dinner.

Copy and complete this word map for **fastidious**:

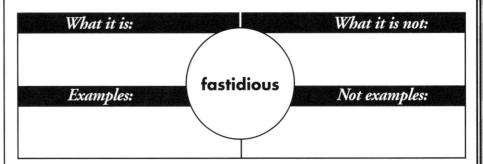

What it is:		*What it is not:*
	fastidious	
Examples:		*Not examples:*

Who is the most **fastidious** person you know?

lunge

verb

to move forward suddenly

The kitten **lunged** at my fish sandwich.

Which of these mean about the same thing as **lunge**?

- to come after someone
- to jump toward
- to lean back
- to sit down
- to attack

Tell about a time when someone or something **lunged** at you. Where were you and what happened?

A Word a Day, Intermediate • EMC 2718 • ©2002 by Evan-Moor Corp.

array

noun

1. a large or impressive group or display
2. beautiful or splendid clothing

An **array** of brightly colored flowers lined the parade route. Soon the queen appeared in royal **array**.

Copy and complete this Venn diagram for **array**:

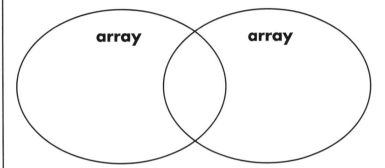

What sort of **array** would you like to wear?

promotion

noun

a move upward in position or grade

My mother's **promotion** at work meant that we could afford music lessons.

Which words mean about the same thing as **promotion**?

- improvement
- advancement
- demotion
- increase
- decline

Give an example of a **promotion** you can receive at school.

A Word a Day

reluctant

adjective

unwilling

The young boy was **reluctant** to jump into the deep end of the pool.

Copy and complete this concept map for **reluctant**:

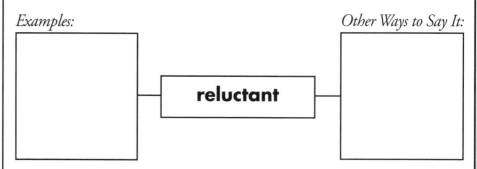

Examples: *Other Ways to Say It:*

reluctant

Give an example of something you are **reluctant** to do.

confront

verb

to meet or face boldly

I decided to **confront** my brother about using my bike without permission.

Which word or words mean about the same thing as **confront**?

- hide
- avoid
- tackle
- deal with
- meet head-on

Tell about a time when you had to **confront** someone about something. What was it about, and what happened?

A Word a Day, Intermediate • EMC 2718 • ©2002 by Evan-Moor Corp.

sensitive

adjective

having a strong awareness of information received through the senses

The new mother was so **sensitive** that she woke up as soon as the infant began crying.

Copy and complete this word map for **sensitive**:

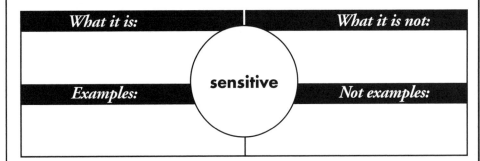

When is it important to be **sensitive**? When doesn't it really matter?

ambiguous

adjective

having more than one possible meaning

synonym: vague

The judge asked the witness to explain her **ambiguous** answer.

Which words mean about the same thing as **ambiguous**?

- uncertain
- confusing
- definite
- unclear
- sure

What can you do to clarify information that is **ambiguous**?

A Word a Day

encumber

verb

to weigh down

The escaping robber was **encumbered** by the heavy sack of loot.

Copy and complete this word map for **encumber**:

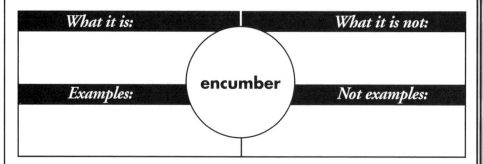

Give examples of other things that might **encumber** you from moving freely.

benefactor

noun

someone who gives a gift of money or generous assistance

Mr. Lawson was one of the major **benefactors** for the new community swimming pool.

Which words describe a **benefactor**?

- helpful
- kind
- stingy
- thoughtful
- selfish

If you could be a **benefactor**, what kind of help would you like to give and to whom?

A Word a Day, Intermediate • EMC 2718 • ©2002 by Evan-Moor Corp.

indispensable

adjective

absolutely necessary

Although we can live a long time without food, water is **indispensable**.

Copy and complete this concept map for **indispensable**:

Examples:

indispensable

Other Ways to Say It:

What is something that is **indispensable** to you?

mortify

verb

to cause someone to feel terrible embarrassment

My brother **mortified** me when he began to sing at my party.

How might someone who is **mortified** feel?

- comfortable
- humiliated
- confident
- humbled
- ashamed

Tell about a time when you felt **mortified**. What made you feel **mortified**?

A Word a Day

finance

1. noun

   affairs related to money

2. verb

   to provide money for someone or something

My mother has been very successful in **finance**. The profits from her investments helped **finance** our family's restaurant.

Copy and complete this Venn diagram for **finance**:

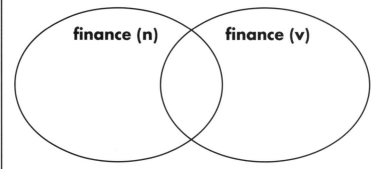

How do you plan to **finance** your education after high school?

bountiful

adjective

more than enough

synonym: plenty

We had a **bountiful** amount of food for Thanksgiving dinner.

Which of these natural elements are **bountiful**?

- crude oil
- pearls
- water
- grass
- trees

What is something **bountiful** in your life?

A Word a Day, Intermediate • EMC 2718 • ©2002 by Evan-Moor Corp.

endorse

verb

1. to give support or approval to
2. to sign one's name

Famous athletes sometimes **endorse** athletic gear. They have to **endorse** a contract to make a legal agreement with a sporting gear company.

Copy and complete this Venn diagram for **endorse**:

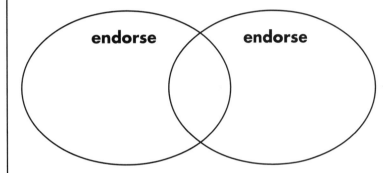

Name some famous people and the products they **endorse**.

idle

adjective

not busy; doing nothing

synonym: lazy

I like to spend my **idle** hours on a rainy day watching old movies.

Would you be **idle** if you were

- swinging in a hammock?
- water-skiing?
- sunbathing?
- canoeing?
- napping?

What do you like to do during your **idle** time?

A Word a Day

descend

verb

to move from a higher place to a lower one

The squirrel quickly **descended** from the top of the tree to the ground.

Copy and complete this concept map for **descend**:

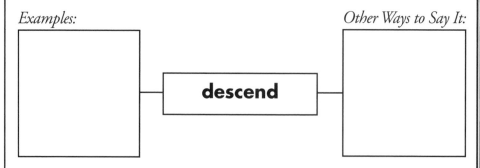

Examples:

descend

Other Ways to Say It:

What is a high place you have **descended** from before?

absorb

verb

to soak up

The sponge **absorbed** all the juice I had spilled.

Which of the following can **absorb**?

- a cloth
- paper
- metal
- wool
- ice

What is the best way for you to **absorb** new information? Do you like to read, listen, or view as a way to **absorb** information?

A Word a Day, Intermediate • EMC 2718 • ©2002 by Evan-Moor Corp.

erroneous

adjective

containing an error

antonym: correct

The prices on the menu were **erroneous**, so we actually paid less than we should have.

Which of the following statements are **erroneous**?

- The United States is one of the oldest nations on Earth.
- New Mexico is one of the states in the United States.
- Texas is the smallest state in the United States.
- The United States is made up of sixty states.
- The United States is in South America.

What do you do when you find out that something you said or wrote was **erroneous** ?

mesmerize

verb

to fascinate

synonym: to entrance

The meteor show **mesmerized** everyone who saw it.

Copy and complete this concept map for **mesmerize**:

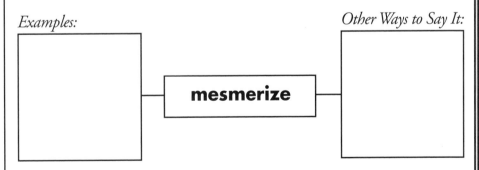

Tell about a time when you were **mesmerized**.

A Word a Day

familiar

adjective

knowing something or someone well

I am very **familiar** with this book because I read it last year.

Which of the following are **familiar** to you?

- chemistry
- the alphabet
- trigonometry
- your best friend
- your classroom

Give examples of something you are **familiar** with.

jubilant

adjective

feeling or showing great joy

synonym: thrilled

The streets were filled with **jubilant** noise as the victory parade passed by.

Copy and complete this concept map for **jubilant**:

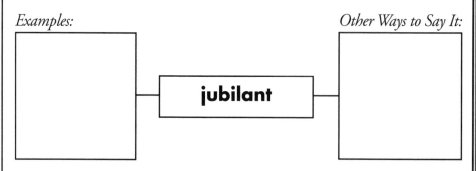

Examples: *Other Ways to Say It:*

jubilant

Tell about something that made you feel **jubilant**.

repose

noun

rest

After a long week at school, I enjoy the **repose** I get each weekend.

Which words mean about the same thing as **repose**?

- calmness
- relaxation
- stillness
- activity
- chaos

Describe the perfect environment in which to find **repose**.

antique

noun

something made a long time ago

The dresser in my great-grandmother's bedroom is an **antique**.

Copy and complete this word map for **antique**:

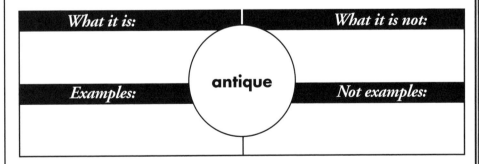

What it is:		What it is not:
	antique	
Examples:		Not examples:

Tell about an **antique** you own or one you would like to own.

A Word a Day

conform

verb

to act or think in a way that follows the rules

I like to sit on the floor, but I must **conform** in school and sit at a desk.

Do you **conform** when you act

- rebellious?
- obediently?
- in a traditional way?
- just like everyone else?
- differently from others?

What is a rule that everyone **conforms** to at school?

fatigue

adjective

the condition of being very tired

synonym: exhaustion

I felt nothing but **fatigue** after the twenty-mile bike ride.

Copy and complete this concept map for **fatigue**:

Examples:

Other Ways to Say It:

fatigue

What types of activities cause you to feel **fatigue**?

A Word a Day, Intermediate • EMC 2718 • ©2002 by Evan-Moor Corp.

infinite

adjective

without limits or an end

There are an **infinite** number of stars in the universe.

Which words mean about the same thing as **infinite**?

- countless
- unlimited
- restricted
- endless
- finite

Give an example of something that is **infinite**.

pucker

verb

to contract into folds

You **pucker** your lips for a kiss.

Which of these parts of your body can you **pucker**?

- your eyebrows
- your cheeks
- your mouth
- your nose
- your foot

Make an expression by **puckering** your facial features.

A Word a Day

adaptation

noun

something that has been changed to fit different conditions

The movie version of *Harry Potter* was an excellent **adaptation** of the book.

Which of these describe an **adaptation**?

- a chick raised by a family of ducks
- a story that is presented as a play
- a poem that is turned into a song
- a song performed by a group
- a ghost story read aloud

Give another example of a movie that is an **adaptation** of a book.

urban

adjective

something that is from the city or related to a city

High-rise buildings and taxis are common in **urban** areas.

Copy and complete this word map for **urban**:

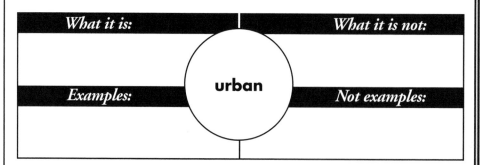

What it is:		*What it is not:*
Examples:	**urban**	*Not examples:*

Describe an **urban** area that you have visited. Would you prefer living in an **urban** setting, or some other type of setting?

A Word a Day, Intermediate • EMC 2718 • ©2002 by Evan-Moor Corp.

converge

verb

to come together

synonym: to join

Main Street and Elm Street **converge** at the center of town.

Copy and complete this concept map for **converge**:

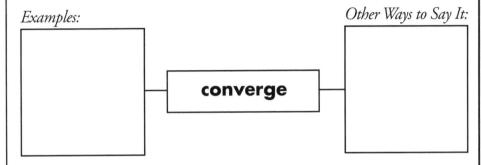

Examples: *Other Ways to Say It:*

converge

Give an example of two streets in your community that **converge**.

sarcastic

adjective

using cutting or bitter words

My feelings were hurt by their **sarcastic** remarks about my haircut.

Which words mean about the same thing as **sarcastic**?

- biting
- ironic
- soothing
- mocking
- encouraging

How would you respond to someone who made a **sarcastic** comment to you? How could you let that person know that you don't like hearing **sarcastic** words?

A Word a Day

esteem

noun

a very positive opinion

synonym: respect

Anita was held in high **esteem** because of all her volunteer work in the community.

Copy and complete this word map for **esteem**:

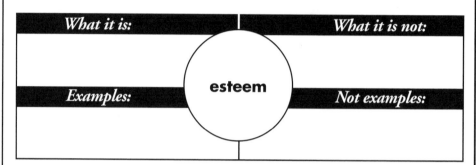

Describe someone you hold in high **esteem**. Why do you admire that person?

cavort

verb

to run and jump around playfully

The children love to **cavort** in the sprinklers on hot afternoons.

Which word or words mean about the same thing as **cavort**?

- prance about
- sit down
- frolic
- play
- nap

When and where do you like to **cavort**?

vehement

adjective

demonstrating strong feelings

She was **vehement** about finishing the project by herself.

Which of the following are **vehement** statements?

- "I will never ever talk to you again."
- "I am absolutely convinced of it."
- "Stop it immediately!"
- "I don't really care."
- "Whatever."

Give an example of something you are **vehement** about.

restoration

noun

the act of bringing something back to its original condition

The **restoration** of the old house took over a year.

Which of these mean about the same thing as **restoration**?

- to let fall into ruin
- to fix up like new
- to run down
- to rebuild
- to repair

Give examples of some places or things that have gone through **restoration**.

A Word a Day

queue

noun

a line formed for waiting

The **queue** to buy tickets wrapped all around the theater and into the parking lot.

Copy and complete this word map for **queue**:

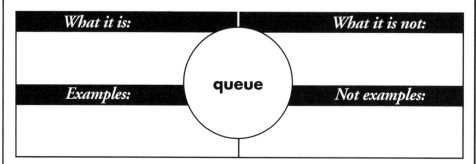

What is the longest **queue** you've ever waited in?

amuse

verb

to entertain

The boys read comic books to **amuse** themselves on the long flight.

Which of these activities could you do to **amuse** yourself while traveling in a car?

- draw
- ride a bike
- read a book
- go swimming
- play guessing games

Give examples of things you do to **amuse** yourself on rainy weekends.

dedicate

verb

to set apart for a special purpose or use

We will **dedicate** the new building for use as a computer lab.

Copy and complete this word map for **dedicate**:

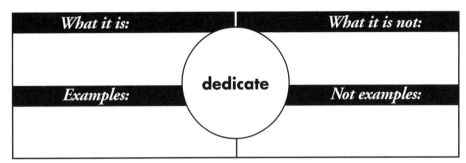

What it is:		*What it is not:*
	dedicate	
Examples:		*Not examples:*

If you had money that you could **dedicate** to charity, what would you do with it?

glare

1. verb

   to stare in an angry way

2. noun

   a bright, strong light

The driver **glared** at us when my mom pulled out in front of him. She didn't see him because of the **glare** on the windshield.

Copy and complete this Venn diagram for **glare**:

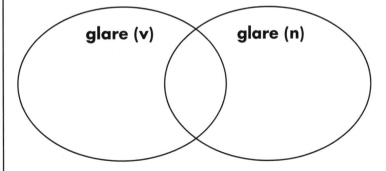

glare (v)   glare (n)

Show how you look when you **glare** at someone.

A Word a Day

utter

verb

to make an audible sound with your voice

We tried not to **utter** a sound as we crept up behind the deer.

Which of these are sounds you could **utter**?

- a sigh
- a thud
- a cough
- a splash
- a scream

What was one of the first words you **uttered** when you learned to speak?

compose

verb

1. to become calm
2. to create by putting together words or musical notes

The musician took a moment to **compose** himself before stepping onto the stage. The orchestra was about to perform the music he had **composed**.

Copy and complete this Venn diagram for **compose**:

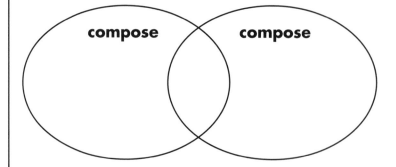

What do you do to **compose** yourself when you are getting too upset or excited?

A Word a Day, Intermediate • EMC 2718 • ©2002 by Evan-Moor Corp.

volunteer

noun

a person who chooses to work without being paid

The Red Cross counts on the help of many **volunteers** to do its work.

Copy and complete this word map for **volunteer**:

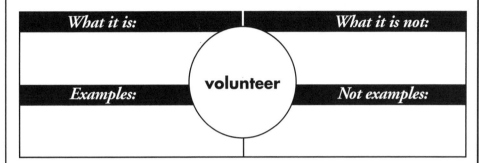

What it is:		What it is not:
	volunteer	
Examples:		Not examples:

What sort of work would you be willing to do as a **volunteer**?

pessimistic

adjective

expecting things to turn out badly

antonym: optimistic

Andrea is so **pessimistic** that she planned for rain during her beach vacation.

Which words mean about the same thing as **pessimistic**?

- excited
- gloomy
- cheerful
- negative
- despairing

Do you think you are a **pessimistic** person? Explain why or why not.

A Word a Day

detest

verb

to dislike very much

synonym: hate

I know that spinach has lots of iron and is a healthy food, but I still **detest** it.

Copy and complete this concept map for **detest**:

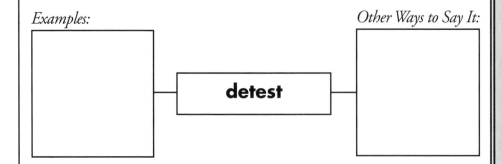

Examples:

detest

Other Ways to Say It:

What is something you **detest**? Why do you dislike it so much?

tolerant

adjective

willing to respect customs, ideas, or beliefs that are different from yours

The key to living in peace is to be **tolerant** of people's differences.

Which words best describe someone who is **tolerant**?

- open
- hateful
- accepting
- gossiping
- understanding

How would you encourage others to be **tolerant**?

A Word a Day, Intermediate • EMC 2718 • ©2002 by Evan-Moor Corp.

ultimate

adjective

final

synonym: last

When the bus reached its **ultimate** destination, only two passengers remained.

Copy and complete this concept map for **ultimate**:

Examples: *Other Ways to Say It:*

ultimate

What is your **ultimate** educational goal?

ventilation

noun

the circulation of air

The cabin was hot and stuffy because there was no **ventilation**.

Which of these help provide **ventilation**?

- a fan
- a sunroof
- new curtains
- open windows
- air conditioning

How do you get **ventilation** in your house?

A Word a Day

anonymous

adjective

from someone whose name is not known

The ancient poem is by an **anonymous** author.

Copy and complete this concept map for **anonymous**:

Examples:

Other Ways to Say It:

anonymous

Why do you think newspapers don't print articles written by **anonymous** writers?

---

know-how

noun

the knowledge of how to do something

A carpenter has real **know-how** when it comes to building things.

Which words mean about the same thing as **know-how**?

- ignorance
- mastery
- difficulty
- ability
- skill

In what areas do you have real **know-how**?

A Word a Day, Intermediate • EMC 2718 • ©2002 by Evan-Moor Corp.

stratosphere

noun

the layer of atmosphere that extends from about eight miles to forty miles above Earth

The air in the **stratosphere** is too thin and cold to breathe.

Which of these might you expect to find in the **stratosphere**?

- birds
- aliens
- clouds
- cold air
- balloons

Do you think it will ever be common to travel through Earth's **stratosphere**? What might that be like?

endow

verb

1. to give money or property to

2. to provide with an ability, talent, or other positive qualities at birth

The company decided to **endow** the college with land to build a new stadium. Their quarterback was **endowed** with the ability to throw a ball for hundreds of yards.

Copy and complete this Venn diagram for **endow**:

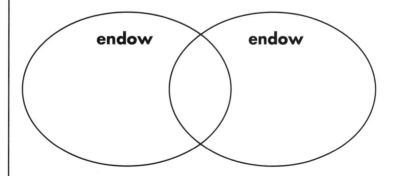

What special abilities are you **endowed** with?

A Word a Day

charisma

noun

magnetic charm or appeal

Kali's **charisma** made her a popular choice for class president.

Copy and complete this word map for **charisma**:

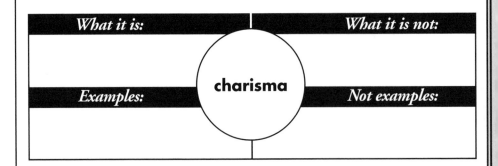

Describe someone you know who has **charisma**.

ancient

adjective

from times long past

The **ancient** pyramids of Egypt still stand today.

Copy and complete this concept map for **ancient**:

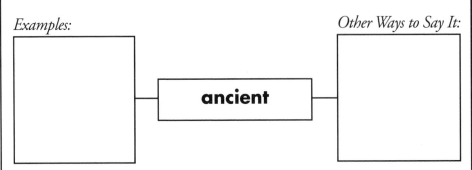

What is something **ancient** that you have seen or read about?

A Word a Day, Intermediate • EMC 2718 • ©2002 by Evan-Moor Corp.

expose

1. verb

   to make something known

2. verb

   to leave open without protection

The detective **exposed** the professor as the mastermind behind the plot. The invisible ink appeared as soon as it was **exposed** to sunlight.

Copy and complete this Venn diagram for **expose**:

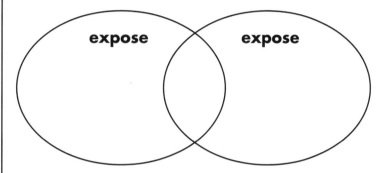

What can happen to your skin if it gets too **exposed** to the sun?

distraction

noun

something that draws one's attention away

The party next door was a big **distraction** as I tried to concentrate on my homework.

Which of the following would be a **distraction** for you when you do homework?

- loud music
- total silence
- the soft hum of a fan
- people talking quietly
- a band playing in the next room

How do you avoid **distractions** when working on something important?

A Word a Day

luscious

adjective

smelling or tasting delicious

The peach mango pie was a **luscious** dessert.

Copy and complete this word map for **luscious**:

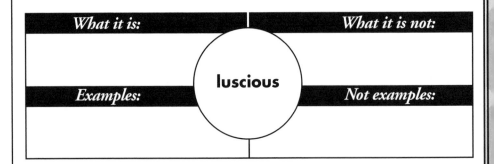

Give some examples of foods you find **luscious**.

forfeit

verb

to give up because of some fault or mistake

We had to **forfeit** the soccer game because we did not have enough players.

Copy and complete this concept map for **forfeit**:

What are some other reasons you might **forfeit** a game?

A Word a Day, Intermediate • EMC 2718 • ©2002 by Evan-Moor Corp.

ignorance

noun

a lack of knowledge

I decided to overcome my **ignorance** of computer programming and take a class.

Which word or words mean about the same thing as **ignorance**?

- complete understanding
- lack of awareness
- comprehension
- misinformation
- cluelessness

What is the best way to overcome **ignorance**?

vain

adjective

overly proud of one's looks, abilities, or accomplishments

antonym: humble

The **vain** actor kept photos of himself all over the house.

Copy and complete this word map for **vain**:

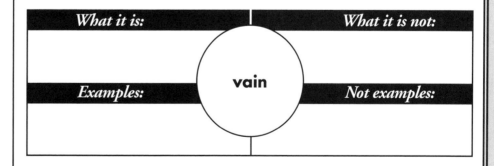

Do you think being **vain** is positive or negative? Why?

A Word a Day

reunion

noun

the bringing together of friends, family, or other groups of people

Family from all across the country got together at our **reunion**.

Which of these might happen at a **reunion**?

- exchanging e-mail addresses
- taking photographs
- doing homework
- sharing a meal
- running

Give examples of groups of people who have **reunions**. Have you ever been to a **reunion**?

shallow

adjective

not deep

It was easy to see shiny rocks at the bottom of the **shallow** creek.

Which of these might be **shallow**?

- a puddle
- a stream
- water in a tub
- the deep end of a pool
- the water on a lakeshore

Where can you find some **shallow** water near your home?

A Word a Day, Intermediate • EMC 2718 • ©2002 by Evan-Moor Corp.

akimbo

adjective

with hands on hips and elbows turned outward

When my mother stands with her arms **akimbo**, I know she means business.

Copy and complete this concept map for **akimbo**:

Try standing with your arms **akimbo**.

banish

verb

to punish someone by making him or her leave a country

The king **banished** the knight after he betrayed his master.

Which of these mean about the same thing as **banish**?

- to welcome home
- to greet warmly
- to send away
- to cast out
- to run out

Why do you think someone would be **banished**? Who can be **banished**? Who can **banish** others?

A Word a Day

calligraphy

noun

beautiful or elegant handwriting

The invitations were written in stylish **calligraphy**.

Copy and complete this word map for **calligraphy**:

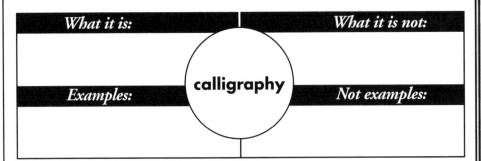

Do you know how to do **calligraphy**? If so, explain how you learned.

essential

adjective

very important or necessary

Sugar is an **essential** ingredient in making cookies.

Which word or words mean about the same thing as **essential**?

- key
- basic
- crucial
- unimportant
- not necessary

What are some **essential** ingredients for making vegetable soup?

formidable

adjective

someone or something to be dreaded

The heavyweight boxer was a **formidable** opponent.

Which of these might be **formidable**?

- an evening at the movies
- a three-hour exam
- a stern principal
- a kind teacher
- a rabid dog

Who is someone that seems **formidable** to you? Why?

esophagus

noun

the tube that carries food from the throat to the stomach

The human **esophagus** is about nine inches long.

Which of these parts of the body work with the **esophagus**?

- the foot
- the neck
- the mouth
- the kneecap
- the stomach

Touch your neck and feel your own **esophagus**.

A Word a Day

sanction

verb

to give approval

City Hall **sanctioned** the building of a new middle school.

Which words mean about the same thing as **sanction**?

- authorize
- support
- permit
- reject
- deny

Would you **sanction** a decision to have school on Saturdays?

pharmacist

noun

a person trained to prepare and distribute medicines

One **pharmacist** handles all the prescriptions filled at our drugstore.

Which of these might a **pharmacist** do?

- count out pills
- use a computer
- take customers' orders
- help customers try on shoes
- tell customers about side effects

What might be difficult about being a **pharmacist**? What might be enjoyable about it?

A Word a Day, Intermediate • EMC 2718 • ©2002 by Evan-Moor Corp.

limber

adjective

capable of being shaped

synonym: flexible

Gymnasts must be strong and **limber** to do all those flips and jumps.

Copy and complete this word map for **limber**:

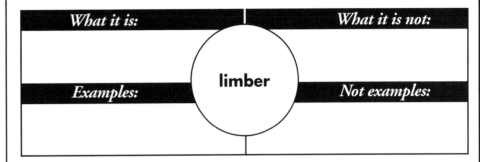

What is something you can do that requires you to be **limber**?

campaign

noun

a series of planned activities to bring about a desired result

The **campaign** for the presidency can last for more than a year.

Copy and complete this concept map for **campaign**:

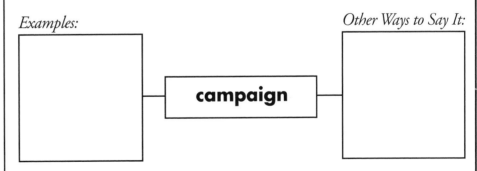

Name some other types of **campaigns** you know about.

A Word a Day

majestic

adjective

grand or spectacular

antonym: inferior

The **majestic** mountains rose up in the distance.

Which words mean about the same thing as **majestic**?

- breathtaking
- magnificent
- average
- splendid
- humble

Mention some other natural wonders that you think are **majestic**.

concoct

verb

to prepare by mixing several different things together

synonym: to combine

I love to **concoct** smoothies with frozen fruit, yogurt, and juice.

Copy and complete this concept map for **concoct**:

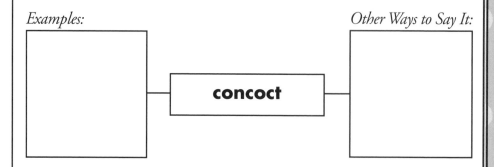

Examples: *Other Ways to Say It:*

Give some examples of things you or your family **concoct**.

A Word a Day, Intermediate • EMC 2718 • ©2002 by Evan-Moor Corp.

ballyhoo

noun

a noisy, attention-getting demonstration or talk

There was a big **ballyhoo** as the home team took the field.

Copy and complete this word map for **ballyhoo**:

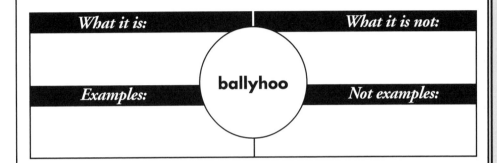

What it is:	*What it is not:*
Examples:	*Not examples:*

Where have you heard a **ballyhoo**?

mischievous

adjective

playful, but naughty

The **mischievous** puppy chewed on all my shoes.

Which words mean about the same thing as **mischievous**?

- kind
- impish
- devilish
- obedient
- thoughtful

Describe a time when you were **mischievous**.

A Word a Day

enunciate

enunciate

verb

to pronounce words
clearly

Our teacher **enunciates** so students who
are learning English can understand her.

Copy and complete this concept map for **enunciate**:

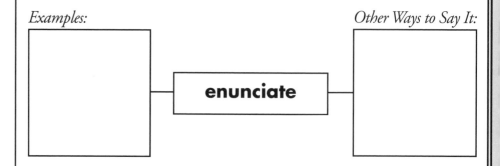

Examples: *Other Ways to Say It:*

Say a few sentences while trying to **enunciate** each word.

intimate

intimate

adjective

1. close and familiar
2. very personal or
   private

My sister's wedding was very **intimate**:
only family and close friends were invited.
I wrote about it in my diary, where I record
my most **intimate** thoughts.

Copy and complete this Venn diagram for **intimate**:

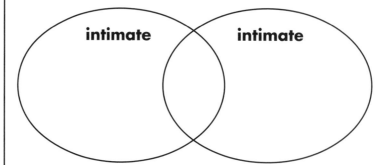

Who is someone you would describe as an **intimate** friend?
Who would you describe as a family friend?

A Word a Day, Intermediate • EMC 2718 • ©2002 by Evan-Moor Corp.

concise

adjective

expressed in a few words

synonym: brief

Isaac's report was **concise** yet packed with information.

Copy and complete this word map for **concise**:

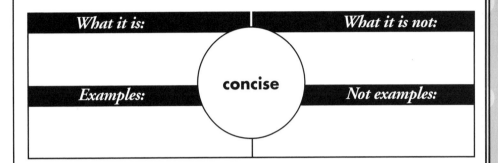

Give examples of some things you've read that are both informative and **concise**.

banter

noun

playful teasing or joking

The backstage **banter** stopped as soon as the rehearsal began.

Which words mean about the same thing as **banter**?

- flirting
- jesting
- ignoring
- heckling
- mockery

Where might you hear **banter** between people?

A Word a Day

gesture

1. noun

   a movement of the hands or head that has meaning

2. verb

   to move your hands or head to emphasize what you are saying or thinking

An international **gesture** meaning "silence" is an index finger pressed to the lips. My mother used it to **gesture** to me during the concert.

Copy and complete this Venn diagram for **gesture**:

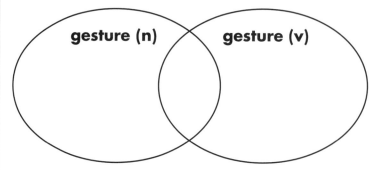

Do you ever **gesture** when you speak? Try saying something, using some **gestures** as you speak.

aquatic

adjective

growing or living in water

The **aquatic** flowers sparkled in the sunlight reflected off the water.

Copy and complete this word map for **aquatic**:

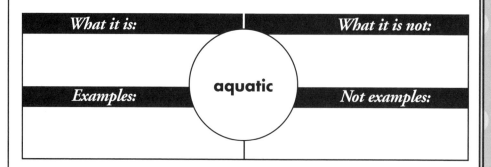

Name some **aquatic** plants or creatures.

A Word a Day, Intermediate • EMC 2718 • ©2002 by Evan-Moor Corp.

enthrall

verb

to hold the interest of someone completely

synonym: to entrance

I was so **enthralled** by the book that I read nonstop for hours.

Which words mean about the same thing as **enthrall**?

- tire
- bore
- enchant
- captivate
- mesmerize

What types of activities **enthrall** you?

dignity

noun

the act of showing one's pride in a confident manner

The Olympic figure skater glided onto the ice with **dignity** and grace.

Copy and complete this concept map for **dignity**:

Examples: *Other Ways to Say It:*

dignity

Do you admire people who have **dignity**? Why?

A Word a Day

buoyant

adjective

capable of floating

The inner tube was **buoyant** enough to support three people.

Which words mean about the same thing as **buoyant**?

- weightless
- unsinkable
- massive
- heavy
- light

Give an example of something **buoyant**.

murmur

verb

to say words in a soft voice

It's OK to **murmur** in the library.

Copy and complete this word map for **murmur**:

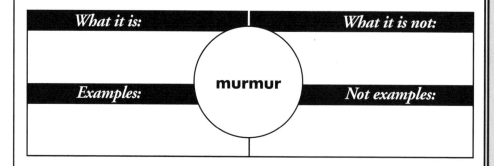

What it is:		*What it is not:*
	murmur	
Examples:		*Not examples:*

Murmur something to a friend. Now listen to your friend **murmur** something.

A Word a Day, Intermediate • EMC 2718 • ©2002 by Evan-Moor Corp.

endeavor

1. noun

   a serious attempt to do something

2. verb

   to make an effort

synonym: to try

He was successful in his **endeavor** to get an A. He planned to **endeavor** to become a scientist.

Copy and complete this Venn diagram for **endeavor**:

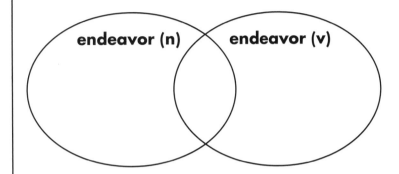

Name some of your own **endeavors**.

triumph

verb

to obtain a great success or victory

The gymnast **triumphed** in the competition and won an Olympic gold medal.

Copy and complete this concept map for **triumph**:

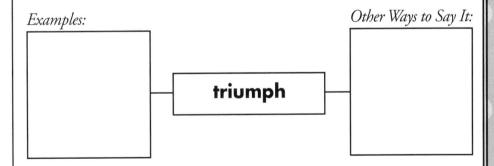

Give an example of one of your own personal **triumphs**.

A Word a Day

circumstance

noun

the time, place, and conditions of a particular event

My grandparents met under wartime **circumstances**.

Which words mean about the same thing as **circumstance**?

- condition
- situation
- feelings
- attitude
- factor

Describe the **circumstances** of meeting someone you know for the first time.

juvenile

adjective

a young person

synonym: adolescent

The marathon had a special prize for **juvenile** runners.

Copy and complete this concept map for **juvenile**:

Examples: *Other Ways to Say It:*

juvenile

At what age do you think you will no longer act like a **juvenile**?

A Word a Day, Intermediate • EMC 2718 • ©2002 by Evan-Moor Corp.

irresistible

adjective

not capable of being resisted

The fuzzy puppy was so **irresistible** that I just had to take it home.

Copy and complete this word map for **irresistible**:

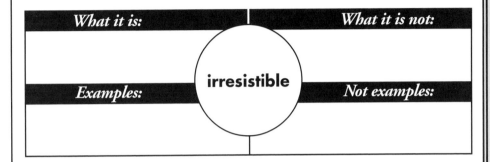

What is something you find **irresistible**?

compel

verb

to drive or urge forcefully to do something

My football coach **compels** me to do my best.

Which words mean about the same thing as **compel**?

- encourage
- require
- permit
- ignore
- make

Who **compels** you to do your best? How?

A Word a Day

enlist

enlist

verb

1. to join the armed forces
2. to get the help or support of someone

My older brother will **enlist** in the U.S. Air Force after graduation.
We had to **enlist** the fire department to rescue our cat from the chimney.

Copy and complete this Venn diagram for **enlist**:

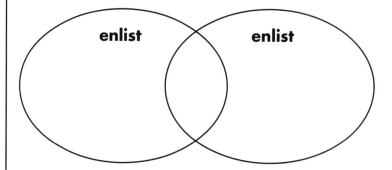

Who can you **enlist** to help you with your homework?

authentic

authentic

adjective

the real thing

antonym: imitation

The sofa was made from **authentic** leather.

Which words mean about the same thing as **authentic**?

- legitimate
- genuine
- phony
- false
- fake

If you couldn't afford **authentic** jewels or leather, would you accept imitations?

A Word a Day, Intermediate • EMC 2718 • ©2002 by Evan-Moor Corp.

nerve

noun

1. a bundle of fibers between the brain and parts of the body
2. courage or bravery

When you touch something hot, your **nerves** tell your brain there's pain, and your brain tells your hand to let go. That firefighter had a lot of **nerve** to run into the burning building.

Copy and complete this Venn diagram for **nerve**:

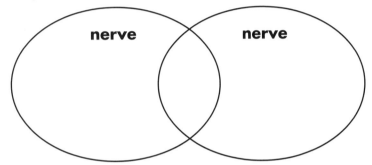

What is something daring that you have had the **nerve** to try?

influential

adjective

having the power to get others to do something without commanding or using force

A very **influential** music teacher convinced me to continue studying the cello.

Copy and complete this word map for **influential**:

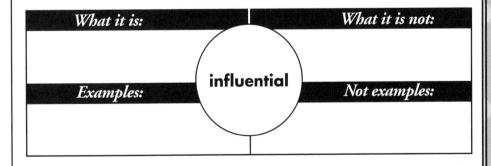

Who is the most **influential** person in your life?

A Word a Day

patronize

verb

to shop at or use the services of regularly

synonym: to frequent

My parents prefer to **patronize** the locally owned market instead of the national chain.

Copy and complete this concept map for **patronize**:

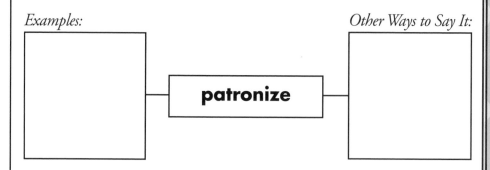

Examples:

patronize

Other Ways to Say It:

What businesses does your family **patronize**?

galaxy

noun

an independent system of stars, gas, dust, and planets

Earth is in the **galaxy** called the Milky Way.

Which of these are part of a **galaxy**?

- dust
- the sun
- a comet
- a satellite
- a milk bottle

Tell the class something you know about the **galaxy** we live in.

A Word a Day, Intermediate • EMC 2718 • ©2002 by Evan-Moor Corp.

courteous

adjective

polite

antonym: disrespectful

It's a good idea to be **courteous** when you speak to your teacher.

Which words mean about the same thing as **courteous**?

- rude
- rough
- unkind
- thoughtful
- considerate

Do you prefer to be spoken to in a **courteous** or a rude way? Why?

burrow

verb

to dig a hole in the ground

Rodents like moles and groundhogs **burrow** tunnels underground.

Copy and complete this word map for **burrow**:

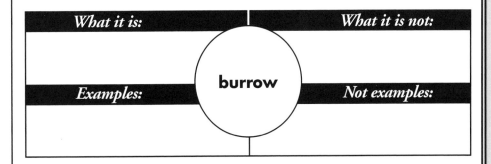

What other types of animals **burrow** in the ground?

A Word a Day

intuition

noun

the ability to guess about something correctly

My **intuition** was right! There is a surprise quiz today.

Copy and complete this concept map for **intuition**:

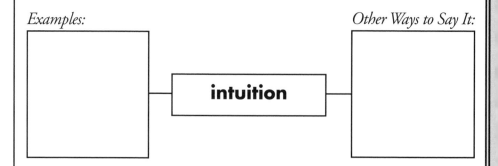

Examples:

Other Ways to Say It:

intuition

Has your **intuition** ever told you about something before it happened?

gorgeous

adjective

very pleasing to look at

synonym: beautiful

The tropical garden was filled with **gorgeous** plants and birds.

Which words mean about the same thing as **gorgeous**?

- grand
- lovely
- hideous
- stunning
- unattractive

What is something in nature that you think is **gorgeous**?

integrate

verb

to make open to all kinds of people

antonym: to segregate

The school board is trying to **integrate** all of the schools in our district.

Copy and complete this concept map for **integrate**:

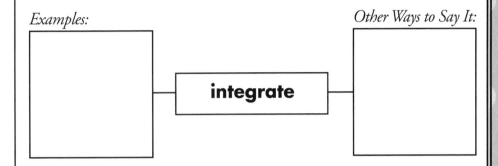

Examples:

integrate

Other Ways to Say It:

Is your school **integrated**? What about your community?

priority

noun

the most important thing at a certain time

My highest **priority** after school is to get my homework done.

Copy and complete this word map for **priority**:

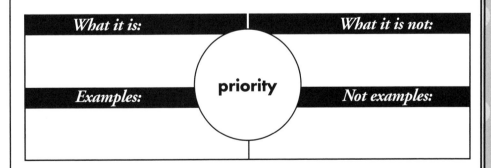

What it is:

What it is not:

priority

Examples:

Not examples:

What is your highest **priority** in today's schedule? What about for this weekend?

A Word a Day

customary

adjective

commonly practiced

In Japan it is **customary** to remove your shoes when you enter a house.

Which words mean about the same thing as **customary**?

- uncommon
- traditional
- strange
- routine
- usual

What is something that is **customary** at your house?

lobby

1. verb

    to try to convince lawmakers to vote a certain way

2. noun

    a hall or room at the entrance

Nature lovers have had to **lobby** the government to protect redwood forests. The **lobby** of the governor's office was filled with protestors.

Copy and complete this Venn diagram for **lobby**:

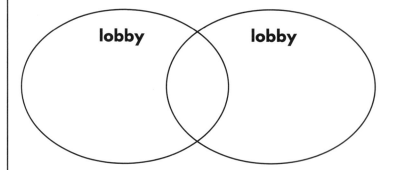

What do you feel strongly enough about that you would **lobby** your government representatives?

charade

noun

a game in which someone acts out each word or syllable of a phrase

You need to have a good imagination or be a good actor to play **charades**.

Which words describe what you do when you play **charades**?

- pretend
- mime
- sing
- talk
- act

Do you like to act or guess when you play **charades**?

jovial

adjective

full of fun

synonym: jolly

Our coach is so **jovial** that even workouts can be fun.

Copy and complete this word map for **jovial**:

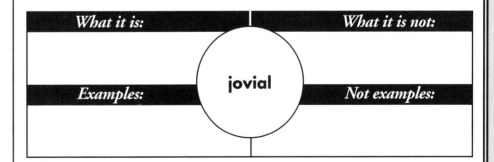

What it is:		*What it is not:*
Examples:	jovial	*Not examples:*

Who is the most **jovial** person you know?

A Word a Day

motto

noun

a short sentence or phrase that expresses a guiding belief

Her **motto** is "Carpe diem: seize the day!"

Which words mean about the same thing as **motto**?

- saying
- slogan
- phrase
- diary
- book

What is your favorite **motto**?

innovation

noun

something newly introduced

The first automobile was a major **innovation** in transportation.

Copy and complete this concept map for **innovation**:

Examples: *Other Ways to Say It:*

innovation

Give examples of other **innovations** and how they changed things.

A Word a Day

ramshackle

adjective

ready to collapse

synonym: rickety

We came across a **ramshackle** cabin on our walk in the woods.

Which word or words mean about the same thing as **ramshackle**?

- in disrepair
- remodeled
- renovated
- run down
- shabby

Describe a **ramshackle** place that you've seen.

confident

adjective

having trust or faith

I am **confident** that I can pass this test.

Which words mean about the same as **confident**?

- sure
- scared
- certain
- fearful
- positive

What is something you feel **confident** about?

A Word a Day

---

honorary

adjective

given as an honor

Famous people often receive **honorary** degrees from universities.

Copy and complete this word map for **honorary**:

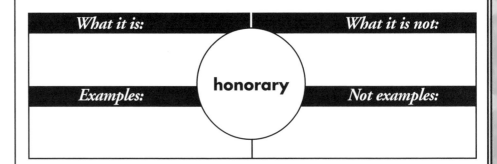

What it is:		What it is not:
	honorary	
Examples:		Not examples:

Think of a famous person. What sort of **honorary** degree do you think that person deserves?

---

literacy

noun

the ability to read and write

Literacy is important for succeeding in our society.

Which of the following activities demonstrate **literacy**?

- reading a sign
- watching a movie
- making a shopping list
- singing a popular song
- sending an e-mail message

Give some reasons why **literacy** is important to you.

overcast

adjective

covered with clouds

synonym: cloudy

I wanted to lie out in the sun, but the sky was **overcast**.

Copy and complete this concept map for **overcast**:

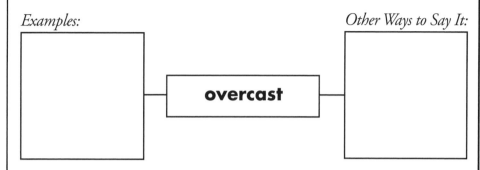

Examples:

overcast

Other Ways to Say It:

Name some activities you cannot do on an **overcast** day. Name some activities you can do.

slovenly

adjective

untidy in dress or appearance

When I returned from camping, I looked a little **slovenly**.

Copy and complete this word map for **slovenly**:

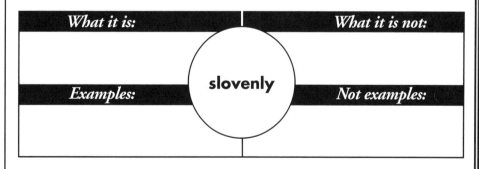

What it is:		*What it is not:*
	slovenly	
Examples:		*Not examples:*

Why might someone look **slovenly**? Do you ever look **slovenly**? When?

A Word a Day

tirade

noun

a long, angry speech

The coach's **tirade** did not help encourage the team.

Which of the following are likely to give a **tirade** from time to time?

- a baby
- a judge
- a teacher
- a teenager
- a military commander

Have you ever had to listen to a **tirade**? Who gave it? What was it about?

oblivion

noun

having been forgotten

The treasure had slipped into **oblivion** until it was rediscovered by explorers.

Which words mean about the same thing as **oblivion**?

- forgetfulness
- popularity
- obscurity
- disuse
- fame

Tell about something that has been rescued from **oblivion**.

A Word a Day, Intermediate • EMC 2718 • ©2002 by Evan-Moor Corp.

Concept Map

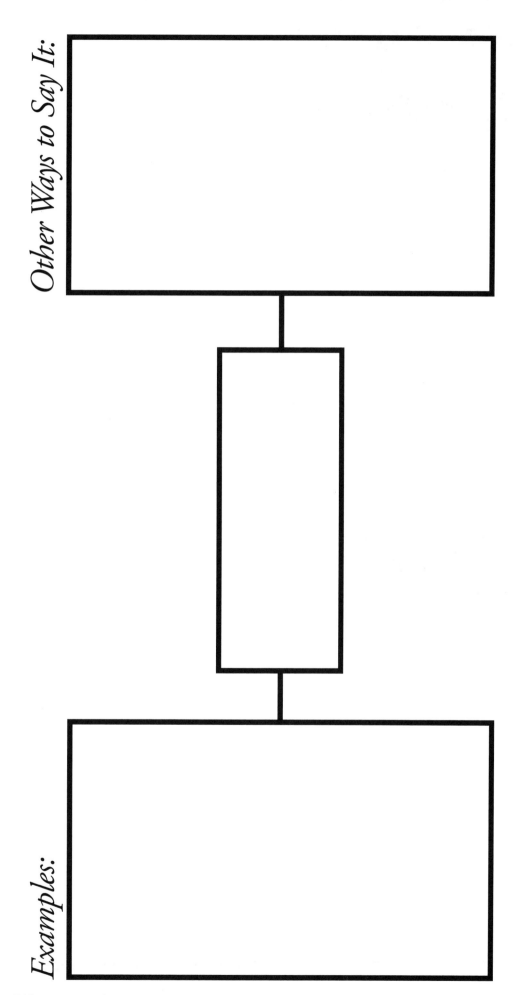

Other Ways to Say It:

Examples:

Word Map

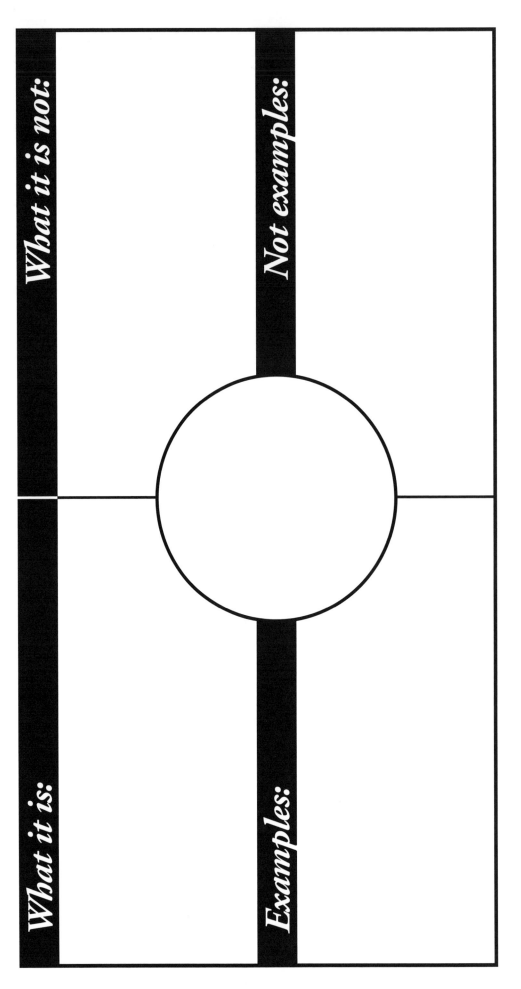

What it is not:

Not examples:

What it is:

Examples:

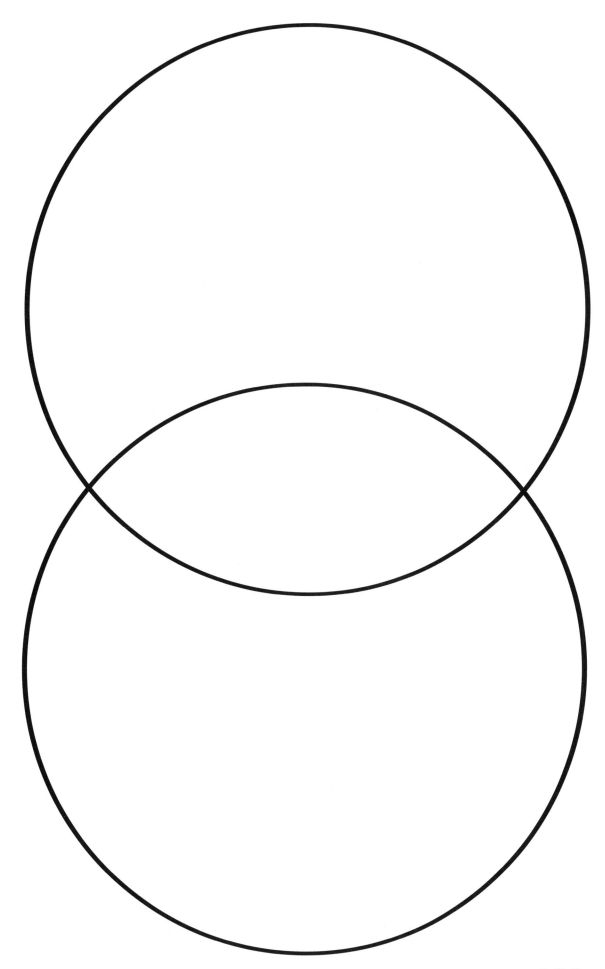

Venn Diagram

Index

abominable 94
abscond 10
absorb 136
absurd 6
adaptation 142
admonish 16
affluent 9
agriculture 23
akimbo 159
amateur 59
ambiguous 131
ambition 38
amuse 146
ancestor 65
ancient 154
annex 82
anonymous 152
antidote 91
antique 139
appease 60
aptitude 74
aquatic 168
array 129
artifact 107
aspire 112
asset 100
authentic 174
automatic 50
avert 127
ballyhoo 165
balmy 75
banish 159
banter 167
barricade 24
bask 75
bedlam 7
belfry 70
belligerent 4
benefactor 132
betray 24
bloat 41
blotch 50
bountiful 134
brawl 14

brawny 83
buoyant 170
burrow 177
bygone 40
calligraphy 160
campaign 163
cantankerous 8
casual 8
cavort 144
charade 181
charisma 154
chronic 98
circumstance 172
classify 15
collate 46
compel 173
compile 114
complement 25
compose 148
comprehend 125
concise 167
concoct 164
condemn 97
condensation 103
confident 183
conform 140
confront 130
congenial 107
congested 49
contemplate 118
contemporary 81
contribute 90
converge 143
convertible 56
correspond 64
corruption 111
courteous 177
coy 64
critique 70
curfew 83
curtail 11
customary 180
dapper 10
deceive 5

deception 126
dedicate 147
defiant 25
dejected 11
denominator 76
deplete 52
descend 136
destitute 18
detest 150
dexterity 42
diagnosis 110
digit 124
dignity 169
digress 12
diligent 26
dimension 65
dingy 38
diplomatic 119
disheveled 95
distraction 155
docile 13
domestic . . . . .6?
dominate 6
dormant 10
efficient . . . .?
elated . . . .
elevate . . . .
emancipate . . . .
emotion . . . .
encounter . . . .
encumber 1
endeavor . . . .
endorse . . . .
endow . . . .
endurance . . . .
enlist . . . .
enthrall . . . .
enthusiasm . . . . . .
enunciate . . . .
erroneous . . . .
esophagus . . . . . .
essential 1
establish . . . .
esteem 14

A Word a Day, Intermediate • EMC 2718 • ©2002 by Evan-Moor Corp.

exaggerate 121
expose 155
exquisite 92
extravagant 104
extricate 122
facilitate 102
falsehood 61
familiar 138
fastidious 128
fatigue 140
fiasco 117
fickle 42
finance 134
flammable 44
flaunt 123
flounder 33
flourish 48
fluctuate 106
foreign 16
forfeit 156
formidable 161
antic 20
iction 71
gid 33
ntier 123
axy 176
ery 17
and 43
ninate 14
ure 168
orous 27
. . . . 147
n 51
eous 178
y 57
rious 13
. . . . 118
s 17
onious 52
rdous 28
y 87
oom 12
isphere 37
nit 9

honorary 184
horde 44
humble 71
humdrum 22
humorous 90
idle 135
ignorance 157
immaculate 45
immerse 101
immobile 126
impartial 57
implore 51
indication 89
indispensable 133
indulge 18
infinite 141
influential 175
ingenious 29
innovation 182
integrate 179
intimate 166
intuition 178
inundate 85
invincible 66
irresistible 173
jaunty 110
jester 120
jostled 87
jovial 181
jubilant 138
jumble 19
junction 45
justify 31
jut 100
juvenile 172
killjoy 55
kindling 62
knickknack 29
knoll 58
know-how 152
kowtow 31
landscape 30
lapse 63
lecture 19

leisure 98
lenient 30
limber 163
literacy 184
loathe 72
lobby 180
loiter 91
luminous 4
lunge 128
luscious 156
majestic 164
majority 127
maneuver 20
mesmerize 137
metamorphosis 108
mischievous 165
moderate 117
mortify 133
motto 182
mundane 113
murmur 170
muse 67
mutter 108
narrative 34
native 94
navigate 61
negligent 79
nerve 175
noxious 54
oblivion 186
obsolete 120
outwit 27
ovation 77
overcast 185
overwhelmed 106
pandemonium 95
paraphrase 67
partial 60
patriot 34
patronize 176
pedigree 97
peer 21
pell-mell 79
penetrate 35

perceive 105
perennial 125
persistent 122
pessimistic 149
petty 115
pharmacist 162
phenomenon 86
ponder 53
priority 179
procrastinate 88
promotion 129
prosperous 84
pucker 141
pulsate 73
pungent 96
quagmire 54
query 109
queue 146
quintessential 114
quizzical 116
radiate 84
ramshackle 183
ravenous 102
rebellion 59
recoil 93
recommend 35
reluctant 130
remedy 7
remote 104
rendezvous 53
renovate 40
replenish 23
repose 139
restoration 145
retaliate 99
reunion 158
rickety 36
rustic 63
sanction 162
sarcastic 143
scavenger 36
scuffle 80
sensitive 131
shallow 158

sincere 72
slovenly 185
snob 49
spartan 93
stagnant 21
stratosphere 153
susceptible 78
tactful 69
taffeta 89
tamper 47
tantalize 81
tariff 68
tarnish 78
tattered 92
taunt 119
tedious 15
temptation 101
tendency 121
terminate 96
terminology 124
timber 113
tirade 186
tolerant 150
tolerate 58
tousled 105
tragedy 73
translucent 99
transmit 39
triumph 171
trivial 37
tuition 47
tumultuous 109
ultimate 151
uncouth 112
undaunted 74
undeniable 80
unkempt 22
urban 142
urge 69
utter 148
vain 157
vanquish 6
vehement 145
velocity 41

ventilation 151
ventriloquist 28
venture 115
versatile 56
vertical 76
vicinity 82
vigorous 48
vital 86
volunteer 149
vulnerable 68
whim 116
whimsical 55
wriggle 111
yearn 46

A Word a Day, Intermediate • EMC 2718 • ©2002 by Evan-Moor Corp.